Ten 2nd Chances

This Doctor Died
and Went to Hell, Why?

Robert Treuherz, MD
with
Claudia Treuherz
Bradley Treuherz
Alan Davenport

For information about this title or to order other books and/or electronic media, contact the publisher:
Two Sisters Writing & Publishing®
TwoSistersWriting.com
18530 Mack Avenue, Suite 166
Grosse Pointe Farms, MI 48236

Hardcover ISBN: 978-1-956879-88-9
Paperback ISBN: 978-1-956879-89-6
Ebook ISBN: 978-1-956879-90-2

Printed in the United States of America
No part of this manuscript is fiction. Only some names of people and places have been changed.
Book cover art and design: Illumination Graphics.
Graphics and formatting: Illumination Graphics.
Author photos: The Treuherz Family Collection.

Some of the artwork featured in this book, including the cover image, was generated with the assistance of artificial intelligence tools.

Preface

When my son Bradley gifted me with this journal from Barcelona along with this Father's Day card on June 18th, 2023, the inspiration for this book was born.

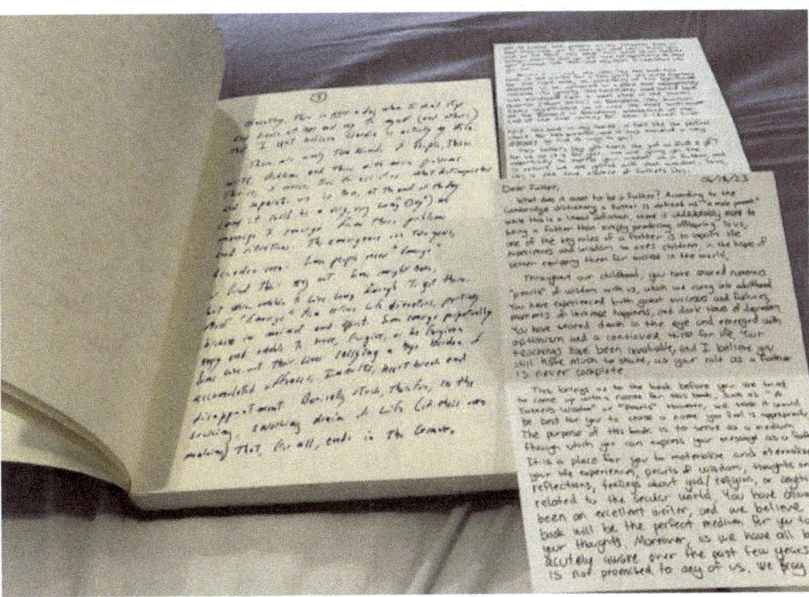

This is the Father's Day card and the journal that my son Bradley gave me as a gift after purchasing it in Barcelona, Spain, asking me to write my story in a book.

Here is what the card says:

DEAR FATHER,

What does it mean to be a father? According to the Cambridge Dictionary, a father is defined as a "male parent." While this is a literal definition, there is undoubtedly more to being a father than simply producing offspring. To me, one of the key roles of a father is to impart life experiences and wisdom to one's children, in the hopes of better equipping them for success in the world.

Throughout my childhood, you have shared numerous "pearls" of wisdom, which I carry into adulthood. You have experienced both great successes and failures, moments of immense happiness, and dark times of depression. You have stared death in the eye and emerged with optimism and continued thirst for life. Your teachings have been invaluable, and I believe you still have much to share, as your role as a father is never complete.

This brings us to the book before you. I tried to come up with a name for this book, such as "A Father's Wisdom" or "Pearls."

However, I think it would be best for you to choose a name you feel is appropriate. The purpose of this book is to serve as a medium through which you can express your messages as a father. It is a place for you to materialize and eternalize your life's experiences, pearls of wisdom, thoughts on life, reflections, feelings about God and religion, or anything related to the secular world.

You have always been an excellent writer, and I believe this book will be the perfect medium for you to express your thoughts. Moreover, as we have all become acutely aware over the past few years, tomorrow is not promised to any of us. I pray that you will be around and present in my children's lives so that they may get to know you and learn from you just as I have.

This book can serve as an insurance policy, ensuring that you will have the opportunity to share your messages with them, and help them to understand who you are.

Believe it, or not, the idea for this book has been in the works for a few years. I was waiting for the right book to present itself, as something of this significance deserves to be contained in a place that appropriately reflects its gravity.

This handmade book was purchased from a small shop in the Gothic Quarter known as *Barri Gotic* in Barcelona, Spain. This location bears significance as it was the first settlement of the Romans in Barcelona, established at the end of the first century BC. When I first held this book in my hands, it felt like the perfect choice for this purpose, and it has traveled a long distance to find its way to you!

This Father's Day gift feels like just as much of a gift for me as it is for you. I am giving you the opportunity to express your wisdom as a father, and in return, I am gifted with that wisdom. To me, this is the true essence of Father's Day.

Thank you for being the father that you are.
With love, your son, Bradley

Photo Gallery

Family trip to Hearst Castle. First time for our dog Max on a beach. We had a ball and he and the boys loved running in and out of the ocean together. I can still see Max jumping in the waves! Left to right, Brian (no shirt), Claudia (black top, cup in hand), Maximus, my mother Beatrix, and Bradley (dark shirt and beard).

Brian and Bradley on the fishing dock near our home in Lake Arrowhead, California, around Christmas 2020. Looks like fish is on the menu!

My wife Claudia and her beautiful daughters. From left to right: Ashley, Claudia, and Amber.

Me and Claudia at Christmas time in 2019 in my mother's house in Toluca Lake.

Bradley, Dad, and Brian having a wonderful Christmas time! This was 2019 at my mother's house.

Contents

Dedication

This book is dedicated to the incredible staff and doctors at UCLA Cardiomyopathy and Transplant Center. This book is also dedicated to the heart donor's family.

The gift of my new heart saved my life, and I am immeasurably grateful to the UCLA Cardiomyopathy and Transplant Center staff and doctors who provided extraordinary care for me during this grueling journey. In addition to being far beyond the leading edge of medicine, they are patient and calming, especially during the most dire and frightening situations. They are the highest echelon of philosophers and educators.

In particular: Dr. Arnold Baas; Dr. Abbas Ardehali; Dr. Daniel Cruz; Dr. Mario C. Deng; Dr. Rushi V. Parikh; Darko Vucicevic, M.D., Dr. Eric S. Hsu; Anca Rahman, ARNP-Advanced Cardiac Failure-Cardiomyopathy NP; and Jonathan George Smith, RN, BSN, CCTC, my Nurse Supervisor and Transplant Coordinator. Also Dr. Boris Larreta at Providence Saint Joseph Medical Center in Burbank, who cared for me and saved my life numerous times before eventually referring me to the UCLA transplant team.

They gave me a new heart and a second chance at life. They trusted me enough to honor and care for this new heart, despite my recent history and treatment for prostate cancer and the traumatic removal of a spinal tumor (meningioma) with chronic spinal damage and a right hemiparesis (partial paralysis and chronic pain). They literally gave me a new birthday. With them, I want to thank many other life savers and miracle workers who on a daily basis give people the gift of a second life.

To those doctors at the initial treating facility who knowingly failed me, and you know who you are, shame on you, and you can do better. Miraculously, I am alive despite your mediocrity, apathy, and in one case— antisemitism and bigotry. I hope, partially, that this book serves as a cautionary tale for both patients and doctors.

More than anything, this book is dedicated to love. It's the love story between me and my wife Claudia which, with God's blessing, is a love that is stronger than death and can transcend time and redefine what it means to be alive.

Best day of my life—me and Claudia on our wedding day, June 13, 2015. Best decision I ever made. Along with God, my ultimate salvation. God saved us, but we also saved each other.

As we enjoyed the idyllic beauty of the California Coast, Claudia and I were blissfully unaware that we were in the calm before the storm that struck just two months later. This photo was taken in 2015, before the near-fatal head-on collision and heart attack, and one month after my cardiac stress test had shown "normal" results.

Three months after the sailboat photo, this was me on Thanksgiving Day 2015, immediately after getting out of the hospital and four weeks after the heart attack, first near-death experience, and two hospitalizations.

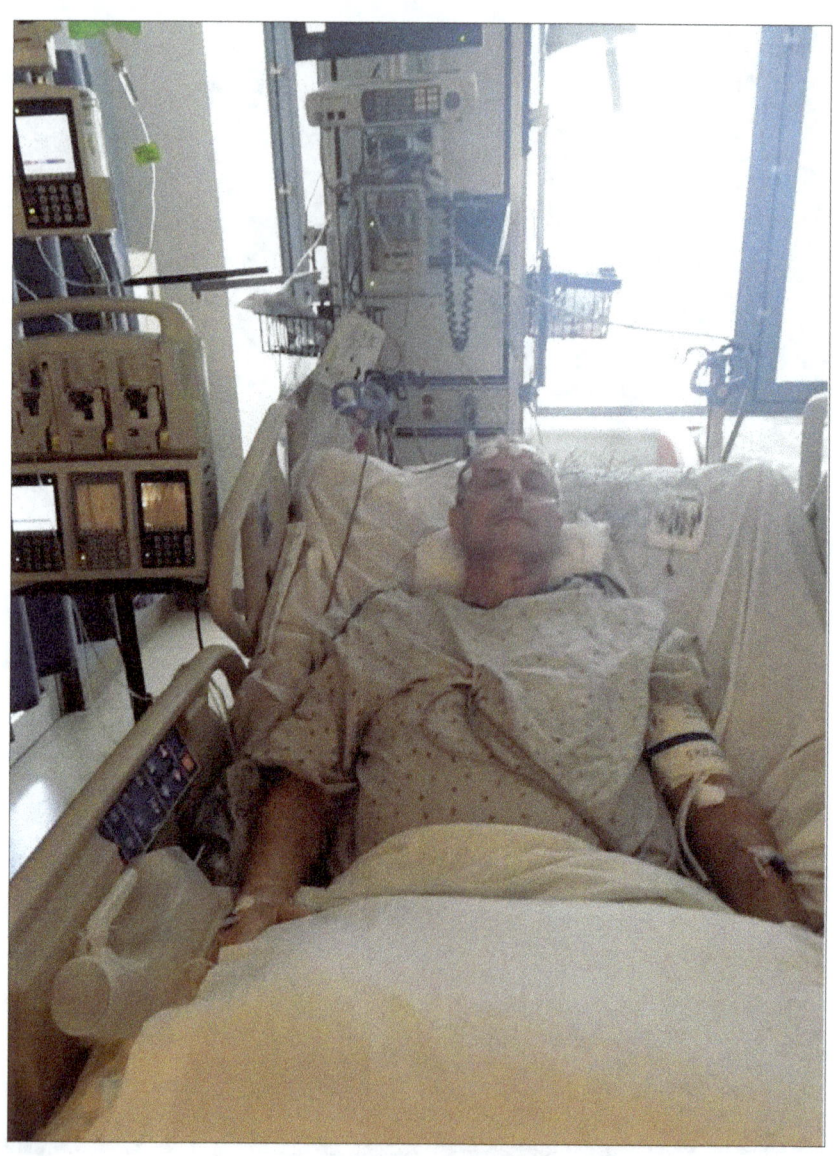

On the brink of death in November 2015.

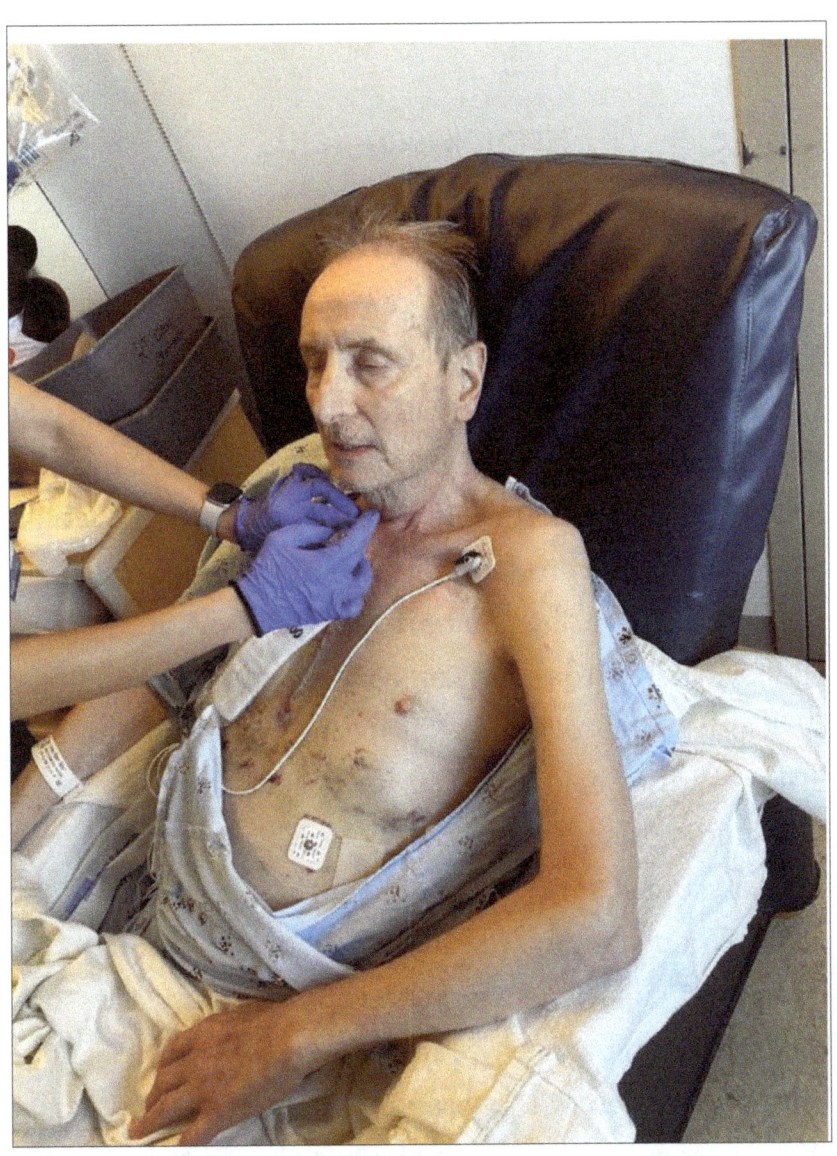

After the heart transplant on February 23, 2024.

Acknowledgments

I wish to acknowledge the selfless and exhausting devotion, sacrifice, love, and dedication from my family. In particular and especially my wife Claudia, my son Bradley, and my mother Beatrix. Without them, I would have died many times over by now. But thanks to them, I continue to live days that are filled with gratitude, love, and joy. Thanks to them, I'm living my best second life.

I also want to thank Elizabeth Ann Atkins of Two Sisters Writing & Publishing® for believing in this project and guiding us to write this book. Our journey began with a request from my son Bradley in a Father's Day card to journal my tumultuous journey through life and death experiences and the transformative lessons I learned along the way. From the beginning, our story resonated deeply with her and we immensely appreciate the expertise and care that she has shared to bring this book into the world.

Introduction

"Father knows best" or "father knows *deaths*"?

I will tell you exactly what it feels like to die, and to come back from death, ten times!

I will tell you what being cursed actually feels like. I will tell you why I am cursed, despite my best efforts to live well and properly.

I will tell you what it feels like to descend straight into Hell, come back out of it, and then repeat the process nine more times.

This book traces my journey from sudden death to the unexpected fall into the terrifying depths of Hell, and back to the heights of a new life made possible by the gift of a new heart from a much younger man.

This birthed a second, liberated, and happy life, as well as my own divine revelations, my own *Divine Comedy*, theological lessons, and a new understanding of grace and faith. This is my journey.

I will also tell you about the love that I share with my wife, Claudia. A love so strong that, with God's permission, defeats death and transcends and even transforms time.

We have become like characters out of Greek mythology, like Orpheus and Eurydice, whose love and the tragic twists made their story one of the most memorable tales in ancient literature.

However, unlike their story, which is a myth—our story is reality.

Orpheus fell deeply in love with Eurydice, a beautiful nymph. They married, but their happiness was short-lived because Eurydice was bitten by a snake, died, and descended into the underworld. Orpheus, a renowned musician, ventured into the underworld to bring her back. His music was so moving that Hades, the God of the Underworld, conditionally agreed to let Eurydice return to the living world.

But ultimately things didn't turn out so well for them as they did for Claudia and me. And in our case, I was the one "bitten by the snake" who initially descended into Hell—and Claudia came in there to save me.

I will tell you and show you the power of real faith, painful soul searching, repentance, redemption, family, and prayer.

I am writing this book, simply stated, because my son asked me to do so as a shared memorialization of my wisdom and experiences. He wanted this knowledge to be available for our family for generations to come. I am tremendously honored and humbled that he asked me to do so. Especially as I lay no claims on possessing any special wisdom or knowledge.

This "wisdom and knowledge" began during conversations with my son as he was growing up. I would take him everywhere with me, including on hospital rounds every weekend, on our long bike rides, and to many other activities. During this time, we would talk about everything from my patients to physics and philosophy and movies and everything else. I was sharing what I had learned about everything throughout my life, and fortunately, he was eager to hear about it and learn from it.

What makes this story so unique is that this led to the unique paradox that every axiom, warning, observation about life, and every bit of medical knowledge I could impart to him, would actually come to a hellish fruition in a series of deadly health problems that happened to me. This deeply affected him and the rest of my family, including my stepchildren.

The combination of horrors that we would have to endure and somehow survive are so extreme and unlikely, that at one point I started seriously wondering, "Have I been cursed?"

I was awed by the irony of being a hard-core scientist who was considering that I had been cursed. The more I considered it, the more solid reasons and criteria I actually found for being cursed.

At the same time, the series of healthcare crises has only served to bring us much closer as a family, especially for me and my wife Claudia. It has redefined what love is, as well as our relationship to time and the nature of life and death. The traumatic experiences I survived opened previously sealed and hidden windows in my mind, revealing new perceptions of human life energy and spiritual beings. This reminds me of what Albert Einstein once said: "Spooky action at a distance."[1]

I will also share what we have learned about staying healthy, living long, avoiding toxic people, living in faith, and being happy every day. Also, learning to appreciate, and making the most of every moment—every NOW moment—of every day.

You will also read chapters written by my wife Claudia, my son Bradley, and my son-in-law Alan Davenport, as they recount these harrowing health experiences from their perspectives.

Thank you for embarking on this journey with us. I hope you take away from this book a newfound appreciation to cherish your life and your loved ones as never before, and believe that miracles do happen.

Robert "Dr. Rob" Treuherz, MD

---

[1] Albert Einstein to Max Born, March 3, 1947, in The Born-Einstein Letters: Correspondence between Albert Einstein and Max Born, 1916–1955, translated by Irene Born (New York: Walker, 1971), 158.

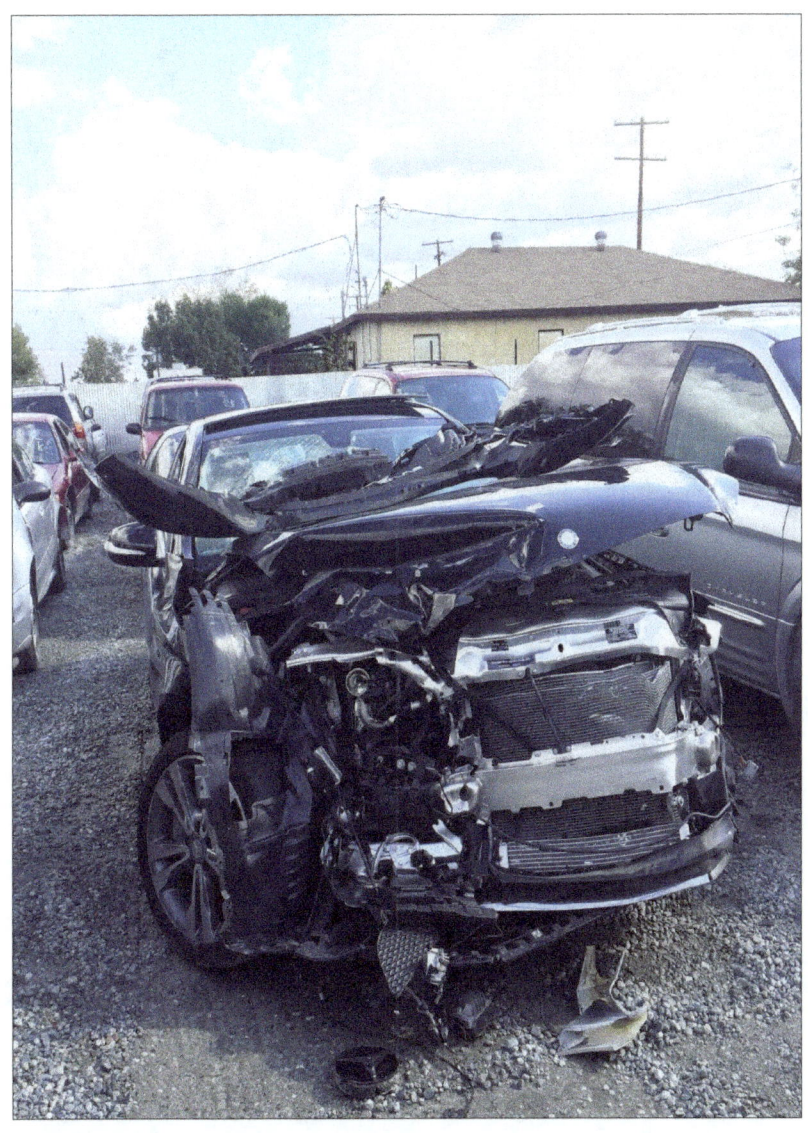

In a blink of an eye, our lives were changed forever. The picture shows our car after the near-fatal collision that precipitated the heart attack, and everything that was to follow, on October 29, 2015.

Chapter 1

My First Near-Death Experience

By Robert "Dr. Rob" Treuherz MD

The head-on collision felt and sounded more like a plane crash than a car accident. My wife Claudia was in the car, and the violent impact fractured her sternum and right clavicle and injured her neck. She screamed in pain.

Even though I smelled the smoke and burning plastic, I didn't realize we were on fire until I saw the flames. They looked like little orange bubbles or pillows spreading out over our heads and around the innumerable airbags that had explosively inflated all around us.

The still familiar and unmistakable smell of burning hair permeated the cabin of the car. The odor was so strong that I could taste the combination of airbag gunpowder, melting plastic, and singeing hair.

Our 120-pound German shepherd, Maximus, had been in the backseat, and was now moving and whining on the floor of the back seat.

I reached over and tried to open Claudia's door.

It was jammed shut. The car was an accordion, and the engine had been ripped out of the vehicle.

Suddenly a loud voice boomed over the speakers: "The car has reported an accident. Do you need assistance?"

I don't routinely use expletives, but I'm pretty sure I did at that moment in asking for help. It seemed like the sirens were blaring instantly.

Actually, they were.

Coincidentally, an ambulance was entering the intersection as we approached it. That's when a young male driver had attempted to beat the ambulance by racing his car through the intersection, but he hit us head-on instead.

After impact, my door opened easily. I rolled out of the car onto the asphalt. I couldn't tell if I was injured or how badly. My only panic-stricken thought was the horror of Claudia's screaming and how to get her out of the car and help her.

The overwhelming and debilitating idea that she may not survive this crossed my mind and absolutely collapsed me from the inside out.

I couldn't breathe and started to panic, feeling like I was going to pass out. I didn't know if my inability to breathe was from injuries sustained in the car accident or if I was having a respiratory arrest from the major trauma. People do stop breathing and die "just" from major trauma.

Up until that instant, we were living an incredibly happy life—with Claudia and I in love like teenagers enjoying every day to the fullest along with our dog Maximus. The events of this day would force me into retirement after a successful forty-year-career as an internal medicine physician at hospitals and clinics in Florida, California, and New York.

And then, from one moment to the next, everything, with the exception of our love, came to a violent, shocking, very prolonged ten-year "pause."

The asphalt felt rough, hot and uneven. It burned the skin of my hands and face. It smelled of gasoline, smoke, and burnt rubber. It felt like I was laying on rocks instead of paved asphalt, not realizing that I was laying on pieces of broken engine, glass, chrome, and steel from my own car.

I became aware of Maximus, whining and licking my face, not realizing that I had instinctively grabbed his leash and gotten him out of the car with me. The paramedic who came over to help me asked, "Is your dog friendly?"

I resisted the impulse to tell the old joke about Max not being my dog in case he bit him.

Our dog Maximus

It was October 29, 2015, a date which for us will certainly live in infamy.

From that moment on, we would be forced to embark on journeys and experiences that would be incomprehensible to the unexperienced. We did not know then that not all of them would be bad and would actually propel us to a different level of living, loving, and experiencing time. Within an hour, we would both be hospitalized, the first of many hospitalizations related to that event that would change our lives forever.

I became aware of the ambulance crew trying to

extract my wife from the car, using the Jaws of Life, a hydraulic rescue tool, and they managed to get her into the ambulance and then sped her away.

It was on that day that I was forced to helplessly watch my wife trapped in a burning car, screaming in pain, facing certain death if she did not receive help immediately.

We were well on our way to experiencing and learning about PTSD.

Another ambulance crew had arrived on the scene, and they were attending to me. I glanced at our car and realized that the unrecognizable smoking heap had probably saved our lives. Insurance adjusters would later tell us that they had never seen a vehicle that looked like that where any of the occupants had emerged alive.

It's funny—some of the things you remember about situations like this. At that very moment, while lying on the concrete, I happened to look up and recognized our neighbor's car from the same street. It was weaving its way through the intersection and the debris from which our accident had just occurred. It literally drove right past me as I was sprawled on the ground.

I suppose, with all the police and ambulance activity, it would've been easy to miss who exactly was involved in that accident. The neighbor who lives directly across the street did not recognize the car. That is how severe the impact and damage was.

The next part of my story involves the ironic intersection of my physical health and my professional experience. You see, years before this in 1996, I had become Board Certified in Internal Medicine, and I was certified in Advanced Trauma Life Support and Advanced Cardiac Life Support. Now, in an instant, I had become the patient experiencing the very traumas that I had been trained to treat.

As I lay there on the asphalt, I was having what is known as an "ST elevation myocardial infarction" or STEMI.

The trauma had caused a total blockage in the main artery that supplies blood to the heart, which is the left anterior descending (LAD) artery. I was having what is known as the "widow maker" of heart attacks. There is a fifty percent chance of death within the first few hours after symptoms start and the survival rate—when this occurs outside of a hospital or advanced care center—is twelve percent. ***Twelve Percent!***

Additionally, I narrowly escaped a full-blown respiratory arrest from the blunt force trauma of the impact of the car accident. In other words, I almost stopped breathing from the shock and died right there and then.

I remember the ambulance ride clearly. It smelled bad, like sweat and sickness. And I wondered where Claudia was in her ambulance.

Would she be taken to the same hospital? When would I speak with her next?

I arrived at that first hospital in less than ten minutes. There, I had time to look at my own EKG and knew I was in deep trouble.

To the credit of that hospital, one thing they did right was to get me to the Cath Lab immediately. For me, it was a sharp downhill decline after that.

I was in shock, and I knew Claudia was badly injured, but I did not know the extent of her injuries. I assumed that she had been hurt worse than me, because the ambulance crews had triaged her first.

Little did I know that I was the one who was dying at that moment of a heart attack. I also did not know until sometime later, that Claudia had been transported to the same hospital.

Starting in the ambulance and continuing in that community hospital, I was liberally dosed with narcotics, which clouded my cognitive abilities and made effective communication difficult.

After two weeks of inadequate care at that local hospital, I rapidly developed the complication of "Failed Stent Syndrome."

This involves stents—small, tube-like devices usually made of metal or plastic which are inserted into narrow passageways in the body, such as a heart artery, to keep them open. The stents that were placed in my heart were **undersized** and **under expanded.** In other words, they were useless to the prolongation of life or restoration of adequate blood flow to the heart. These stents were barely enough to keep me suspended between life and death.

Had the first hour of care been handled properly, I should have gotten away with only minimal damage. I would have been able to get up and walk out of the hospital to resume my normal life within weeks. However, these undersized and under-expanded stents caused me, as precious time was wasted, to damage my heart wall. As a result, the medical team gave up on me having any chance of survival. In other words, I suffered irreversible damage, which made me a "dead man walking."

Instead of improving, I was deteriorating every day and knew for certain if I stayed in that hospital, I would never leave alive.

At no time during this hospitalization did anyone recommend transferring me to a higher-caliber facility for consideration of a heart transplant.

All the signs of my deterioration and criteria for a "Failed Stent Syndrome" were there, yet **none** of the cardiologists would acknowledge them. They had given me up for certain death because they had made up their minds that I was going to die, and that was it.

I knew they had medical options, and they refused to try any of them because they believed nothing would make any difference.

This fatalistic attitude was decided by the lead cardiologist on their team and **no one** in that hospital—no intern, resident, or nurse—would dare to state the obvious to the lead cardiologist because they were all intimidated by him. They would rather let a patient lay there and wait to die than risk pissing off this cardiologist.

"Do something, please!" I yelled at him. "I am dying! Please help me! I know you have options; do something!"

In front of my wife, this "cardiologist" responded by humiliating me and yelling back, "What do you expect? You had a heart attack!"

Then he added, "You are not a cardiologist."

During the course of the two weeks or so that I was at that facility, every day was pretty much a new version of going downhill. Each day, a different intern or resident would come in, and I would ask questions.

"I don't know," he or she would say. "I have to ask the attending." Or, "I don't know. I'm going to be a dermatologist."

They would never provide any meaningful answers or information about a plan to save my life.

Every day I woke up, if I could sleep at all, seated in a chair, breathing through pursed lips, which were purple from lack of oxygen. The nurses recognized that I was in trouble the entire time.

The daily nursing notes had comments like, "Patient still having chest pain" or "needs more medication for pain" or "cannot breathe" or "needs more oxygen." The medical records obtained later by my attorneys verified all of the above.

Yet, the interns and residents would write, "Continues to improve, best day ever, says he feels fine."

Then the physical therapists would write a note like, "increasingly unable to walk without more supplemental oxygen and more assistance" or "copious pulmonary secretions still not clearing as per respiratory therapy."

These conflicting communications clearly showed a serious discrepancy in expectation from the cardiologist leading the case versus his interns and residents. They were only trying to survive and get to the next rotation without rocking the boat and eventually graduate from medical school without a problem.

For me, however, this was not an abstraction. This was my life and my family, and I had an obligation to myself and my family. I needed to pull myself out of this death spiral and get myself to a facility that gave a damn and was going to make an effort to save me.

I survived long enough to transfer myself to another facility.

This sounds so casual. But it is a big deal to get from one hospital to another when the patient is not stable.

It is actually a very big deal when the medical doctor— who is also the patient—signs himself out of the hospital against medical advice. Incredibly, this was something I would find myself doing eventually from a hospital in Florida in order to stay alive and fight for my life.

Among other considerations, there's the real possibility that if you sign out of the hospital against medical advice, known as AMA, that your insurance may refuse to cover the hospitalization!

I know that my having good insurance also contributed to this first hospital wanting to hold me there. A nurse administrator there actually told me that for every ten patients they had, only one had insurance, and that I was a very precious asset to them. I choose my words carefully when I say I was an asset, not a patient. Patients are meant to receive proper medical care that is intended to save and prolong life. I did not receive such care at this hospital.

Unbelievably, she confidentially shared with me that I would never be "stable" in that hospital because they would not let me leave. A lifesaving example of when to listen carefully, and when not to listen to so-called authority.

Sadly, to add insult to injury, and I don't know how large a role in my care this played, but it wasn't until some months later that we learned that my attending cardiologist at that initial hospital had made some vicious, antisemitic remarks about me. This cardiologist is no longer working there, and it is unclear if he is seeing patients at all.

My wife and I were shocked by this, and I guess we were a little naïve. Current world events, however, sadly only make the remarks that were relayed to us more believable.

There is a slightly morbid humorous component to this, and it speaks to the concept in medicine of "knowing your patient." This refers to really knowing your patient: his history, past medications, past family history, etc. A patient's religion is typically listed at the very front of the chart, on what is known as the "facesheet."

What's humorous about this, is that I happen to be Roman Catholic. Ironically, because of his lack of interest in "knowing his patient," he simply assumed that I was Jewish and took it away from there. He was literally too lazy to open the chart and simply look at the face sheet! This is a cover sheet in a patient's file that summarizes a patient's personal and demographic information, and it provides medical staff with a snapshot of important information about the patient.

My stepfather taught me when I was young to never judge anyone for anything that is out of their control.

That included race, color, sexual orientation, etc. This has served me well and blessed me with many friends.

I was also very acutely aware from my own professional observations and well-established national statistics that mismanaged healthcare in this country is the *third* leading cause of death, second only to heart disease and cancer. Some studies like the one from Johns Hopkins, estimate that medical errors contribute to 250,000 to 400,000 deaths annually—which would place them right after heart disease and cancer.[2]

As such, I recognized a deathtrap when I had the misfortune to fall into one. Only by the narrowest of margins, and with my wife's help, did I manage to escape that place alive. I then transferred myself to another facility to stay alive.

After transferring to the second facility, they immediately began using all available options to save my life. Unfortunately, due to the extensive damage, the process was far from smooth.

At this new facility, I had undergone a complicated and risky procedure to repair the stents. For the following days, my wife refused to leave my side, except for the moments where a shower and change of clothes were

---

[2] Martin A. Makary and Michael Daniel, "Medical Error—The Third Leading Cause of Death in the US," *BMJ* 353 (2016): i2139, https://doi.org/10.1136/bmj.i2139.

necessary. I was on the phone with her on one such occasion when, suddenly, I found myself sinking into a dreamlike state, with veiled and foggy memories of my body being surrounded by people doing something to every part of me. They were sitting on my chest, pushing hard to restart my heart, with everyone excited and yelling. These images were frightening yet disembodied at the same time. I distinctly remember the smell of my own flesh burning as I was shocked by the defibrillator over and over again.

Oddly enough, once again, none of this seemed real or that it was happening to me and none of it caused me any pain or fear.

As an internal medicine doctor, I quietly recognized that I was being "coded" because my heart had become pulseless in a fatal heart rhythm called Ventricular Fibrillation. This is a severe cardiac rhythm disturbance where the lower chambers of the heart, the ventricles, contract in a rapid and uncoordinated manner, leading to the heart's inability to pump blood effectively. This condition is an emergency, and can result in collapse, loss of consciousness, and sudden cardiac death if not treated immediately.

I have murky, dreamlike memories and visions of this event fading in and out. I have no idea how long this continued. What happened next was much worse.

That's when everything went dark. Really dark and

really cold. If you have ever had the opportunity to tour a cave system, and they turn off the lights to show you what total darkness looks like, then you know what I am talking about. It's an unusual experience. Very dramatic and disturbing.

However, before the "darkness," there's the sinking. The out of control, startling, falling sensation that accompanies an empty, lonely, and departing feeling. Like watching someone who cannot swim fall into the water and helplessly squirm and gyrate, while sinking deeper and deeper, unable to stop.

The sinking starts slowly, like you've stood up too quickly from a chair and feel a little dizzy. Then it transforms into an irresistible, very rapid, downward slide into the darkness. Like a rollercoaster after it's gone over its highest part, then plunges downwards—except this one keeps falling into a kind of cave-like, infinite abyss and it continues to speed up as you're sinking.

At this point, you are still acutely aware of the smells in your physical environment. And you can hear quite clearly whatever is happening around you. Later some senses fade very rapidly, and the sense of sight is completely gone. Hearing continues for a **very** long time, although it gets weaker and weaker as more time passes.

For a while I had the weird impression that I was holding onto something, like a downward-curved cold, steel handrail which eventually faded away. Maybe I was holding onto the bedrail. I thought I had lost all my senses and eventually realized, or became aware, that I had also lost my body.

I realized that whatever was left of me was "sinking" backwards, away from everything and everyone, **including away from myself!** What was worse even than the darkness and cold were the absolute and constantly increasing loneliness and separation from everything, including God.

I was reduced to an *awareness* that was fading away rapidly and becoming fainter and fainter. The only one of my five senses that remained was my hearing; I heard Claudia's voice very clearly:

"Please, baby!" she cried. "Come back! I know you can do it! Come back!"

Desperation rang in her voice: "Please do not leave me alone! Please come back to me! I cannot do life without you!"

These are images that I created using AI to convey my descent into Hell as Claudia begged and pleaded with me and God for me to come back to life.

"God!" she yelled. "God please bring him back!"

Then rage mixed with terror burst out in a threat: "Don't make me come in there and get you!" She really meant it.

I would rather die 10,000 deaths, more if I could, than allow her to be left alone in life without me, or let her see what I was seeing, or wind up where I was in that moment.

At this point, there was no more "I" or "me," no "doctor" or "father" or "male or female," just the slightest mist of a disembodied awareness struggling to find what direction Claudia's voice was coming from in this infinite and constantly increasing formless and disorienting void.

Claudia was the only light and warmth in the darkness.

Oddly, the closer I got into that deep void, the more I felt that I was becoming part of something else, something much larger, something timeless, and infinite. Something crowded, malevolent, compressed, and desperate.

I glimpsed what appeared to be two massive, almost obelisk-like braids or ropes of fiery dark gold, like two flaming golden rivers, intertwined, yet moving in opposite directions.

In the total darkness, one of them emitted an eerie light that was throbbing and glowing in a repulsive way while slithering like a giant snake. It gave off a sickening smell, like burning hair or flesh. Somehow, I recognized that smell as the residual odor from my own flesh being burned by the external electrical shocks and defibrillation as the medical team used paddles on my chest during the cardiac arrest code. Or at least that was what I thought it was.

Like the poles of a battery, these ropes seemed to have their own polarity—one positive and one negative. At least, that was how I perceived it.

Except, however, that negative polarity associated with one of the rivers of fiery gold, had a much darker color to it, and the negative polarity wasn't so much electrical as it was a force, a feeling that was vibrating and reeking of pure evil and terror.

The other strand, in contrast, was strangely unavailable to me. It was a much lighter color, a more beautiful, flowing, streaming river of liquid gold. It felt inviting and radiated warmth and affection, and had a uniquely sweet, otherworldly smell of love and warmth.

For some reason, that "positive" river of gold was out of focus, out of reach, and fuzzy. At the same time, I had uncomfortable clarity and a sharp focus on the "negative" river. Somehow, I knew that this negative river was the path to my final destiny, and there was little I could do to change that.

In that pure darkness, each of the two vast ropes or braids of gold, started from infinitely far away, and continued, also infinitely far away in the opposite direction.[3] It was exactly as Marcus Aurelius, in *Meditations*, had described time itself.[4]

These strands appeared to be moving, in what I can only guess to be at an impossibly fast speed—maybe even the

[3] Marcus Aurelius, *Meditations*, translated by Gregory Hays (New York: Modern Library, 2003).

[4] Marcus Aurelius, *Meditations*, translated by Gregory Hays (New York: Modern Library, 2003).

speed of light, in opposite directions. It was beautiful, and horrible, and mesmerizing at the same time.

The darker strand was pulling at me, drawing me into it in a creepy, unsettling, and frightening way.

Stranger still, is that these humongous, flaming, frantically, moving intertwined rivers of gold, moved in complete silence. It was as though they were in space, where there would be no sound. I felt the urge to cover my ears, at the same moment that I realized that I had no more body or ears at that point. I was, literally, just pure thought.

There was a millisecond of bone chilling, terrifying clarity, where I could see clearly, and almost close up what the strands looked like; it was as though for a millisecond the river froze so I could get a look at it. The dark river, which was clear to me, was made of horribly distorted **faces!**

To make a wild understatement, this did not feel warm or welcoming or safe; this was palpably malevolent. This only renewed my efforts to locate the direction that Claudia's voice was coming from.

The void was cold and getting colder, but not in the sense of temperature (a feeling that I still struggle to understand or describe) at the same time that it impossibly kept getting darker and darker with a simultaneous feeling of dread, foreboding, and terror.

At this point—exhausted, scared, and falling apart—all I could do was keep struggling to hold onto that fading awareness and somehow direct it towards Claudia's voice.

Without her voice, I would have had no compass or heading to direct me away from the descent into oblivion. Again, she was the light, every other direction was leading to the irreversible darkness, terror and emptiness.

I literally felt myself trying to "swim" amidst this fading awareness, almost on a molecular and spiritual, if not physical, level, towards her voice.

It's hard to describe that moment when you realize there aren't going to be any angels, or tunnels of light, friends, or deceased family members happily waiting to greet you. Not even your dog.

That's the moment you realize that you are going to Hell.

To make matters worse, from that very first time, I have had a dreadful, persistent, quiet sense of resolve that this was always going to be my destiny, no matter how hard I worked on changing that.

The realization is crystal clear that, despite having lived what I thought was a "good" life—having devoted my life to helping others; following a noble profession (I would spend Christmas Eve in the ICU with dying patients so they wouldn't die alone); being what was considered by many an excellent diagnostician; and being a devoted, "always there" hospital physician—that I was doomed to Hell.

While not at work, I would devote every spare moment to my children. All of this, notwithstanding, it was becoming increasingly clear that this would be my destiny.

What a horrible and depressing realization that, after living like this, my destiny at the end was to go to that part of the universe and fall into the part of the river of time which was reserved for failed souls.

That river of time, to paraphrase Marcus Aurelius' *Meditations*, moves from an infinite abyss in the future to an infinite abyss in the past and all things that have ever been or will ever become a forgotten part of that river.

I apologize for digressing from the story for a moment, but I think this is the perfect time, given the subject. In *Meditations*, Marcus Aurelius goes on to ask, "What is it that I am?" Meaning, what is it that any of us are? He answered his own question with "a little flesh and breath, and the ruling part."[5] He goes on to elaborate how the flesh and breath vanish forever quickly, but the ruling part, as he puts it, is the only part that has the potential to leave something behind that could last forever.

Interestingly, he also states that we all know that we have something we must do before we die. However,

---

[5] Marcus Aurelius, *Meditations*, translated by Gregory Hays (New York: Modern Library, 2003).

the vast majority of us die, having procrastinated long enough that the small amount of time allotted to us is gone before we ever get to complete that task.

He uses the term "procrastinated" in the worst, most insulting way possible. Meaning, we allow our lives to be wasted, focusing on thoughts about silly, petty, unimportant things that have no value and are merely distractions.

Perhaps, in part, I was allowed these *Ten 2nd Chances* in order to write this book, so that component which represents my "ruling part" will "live on" by means of what I write in this book. This now, is my prayer, my mission, and my goal.

I can't think of anything more relevant to the process of dying than what one thinks about while dying.

The desolation, darkness, strange malevolence, and terror combined with the realization that I was going to be alone—separate from Claudia, my family, all divinity, all hope, and everything that I had ever been or would ever be as well as those that I loved, still makes me break into tears when I relive it.

It was a sinking feeling that kept getting scarier and darker and colder and more terrifying with every moment. What's worse is that it's not a fast feeling like flipping a light switch. It has an endless, timeless quality to it.

It can't be overstated; this was a total separation from people, my beloved family, from God, from myself, from gender, from being a doctor. Yes, this was death, and a very dark one at that. Even worse than realizing this was a horrible death, is realizing that this was Hell. Hell is real and I was there.

I so much wished to not be there; I desperately wanted a second chance. I wanted to be alive; I wanted more time with my wife; I wanted to see my sons; I wanted to be a grandfather. I wanted and desired what was no longer being offered. It seemed too late, until her voice—Claudia's voice—pierced the darkness, as if in a dream. I had to find her. I had to find my way back. I was weeping although I had no physical presence. I was crying out to God, pleading, begging for mercy and for more time to get it right and avoid being sent to Hell again.

The only thing more intense than the darkness and the "burning" cold, is the realization of how ultimately insignificant you are, and have always been in the greater scheme of things. Every part of your identity is being stripped away and slowly disintegrating as you're sinking in a very terrifying place that you shouldn't be going toward.

It was the antithesis of what anyone would imagine as a reward for a good life or death.

I continued to hear Claudia's voice, but it was

becoming increasingly more faint. The darker and deeper I fell into that terrifying blackness, the harder it became to hear Claudia saying:

"Come back, come back, don't leave me! I'll come back in there after you!"

I could also hear my mother, who was crying and praying. This broke and destroyed her as much as it did any of us. And like the rest of us, no one ever fully recovers from an emotional trauma like this.

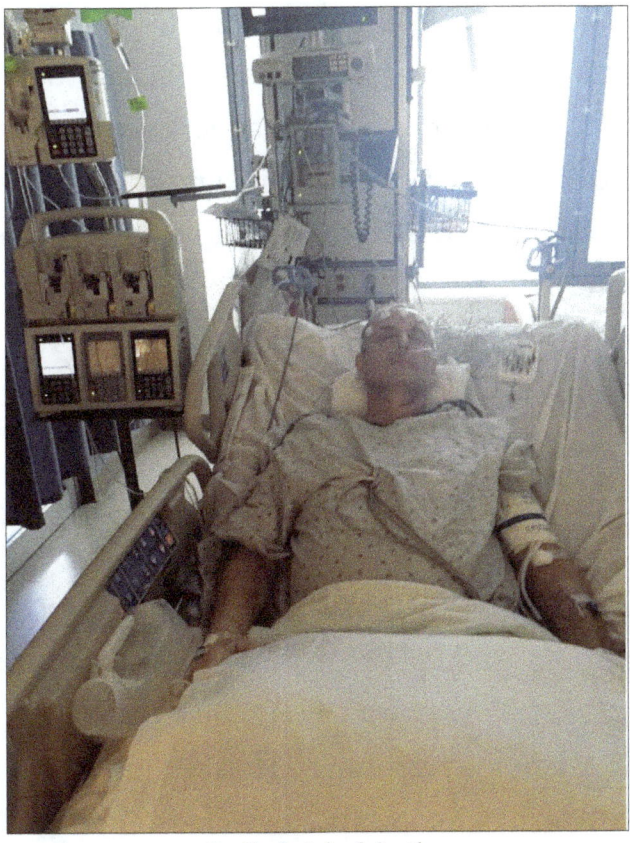

On the brink of death.

Meanwhile, I kept sinking into Hell.

Why is this happening to me? I wondered.

Strangely, at that moment, I remembered a patient I had stayed with in the ICU on Christmas Eve. She was not expected to live. I stayed with her so she would not die alone overnight. Miraculously, she experienced a complete recovery virtually overnight and woke up with stable vital signs.

This patient had become overwhelmed with pneumonia and sepsis, and to this day, I have no logical explanation as to why she improved in that timeframe. She was having all the usual drastic, end stage medications and she was on a ventilator, but the only thing that seemed to make any difference was my sitting there and praying for her.

Many other people were praying for her as well. Her initials are A.M. and today she lives a happy, healthy life in Fort Lauderdale, Florida.

As a classically trained physician, I was on call thirty-six hours straight every third day at Mt. Sinai in New York City. I had completed a one-year rotating internship in Family Practice at St. Joseph Hospital in Yonkers, followed by three years of Critical Care/ Internal Medicine training at Mount Sinai, Beth Israel, and the Bronx VA hospitals. I had also done my OB/GYN training at the Metropolitan Hospital in Manhattan, and one quarter by invitation in an exchange program, during which I completed a surgical rotation at Hospital Boucicaut in Paris, France.

During our years of relentless, exhausting training, the other interns, residents, fellows, and I would routinely hallucinate from fatigue—seeing bodies that had died the night before during codes, floating around in the elevators, and hearing their voices. We could see them and smell their gowns, stained with vomit and medications.

Were these sleep-deprived hallucinations? Some kind of "mass hysteria?" We never knew, and we will never know.

As part of my soul searching, I speculated that maybe I went to Hell because I had been too tired/exhausted to take better care of some of my patients who died. It haunts me to this day.

Maybe the reason I went to Hell was because I had made preventable mistakes without realizing and it cost people's lives.

As you can imagine, I had substantial and painful thoughts on why I went to Hell, and why that was my fate at that time. I thought unless I found and/or took some specific actions to prevent that, I would end up back in Hell when I died "again." I was terrified. I did not have the answer. I started a deep soul search.

I started to think that if I changed my deeds, if I gave more, if I was a better doctor, if I was a better husband, a better father, a better son, a giver, etc., I would inherit Heaven. I was **wrong**.

There was nothing I could physically do to prevent my soul from going to Hell again. Yes, God reveals to us the mistakes we have made along the way through soul searching, and I certainly made some along the way, but I would realize later that redemption doesn't come from anything we can do. I believe that only through Christ can we be redeemed. I did not understand that at all. That's why it says in the Bible, Ephesians, 2:8-9 (NIV): "For it is by grace you have been saved, through faith—and this is not from your-selves, it is the gift of God—Not by works, so that no one can boast."

One day it all clicked. If this sounds preachy, it is not intended to. My journey towards redemption was a struggle to understand what it meant to be forgiven. God doesn't force us into anything. We are given free will. All I had to do is receive the gift God gave us through the sacrifice and suffering Christ endured on the cross to pay for our sins. To pay for **my** sins, so I wouldn't have to go to Hell.

Accepting Jesus Christ as my redeemer, establishing a personal relationship with Christ (which I would come to understand later) was the only path to avoiding Hell and attaining salvation.

When you conclude that your life is very close to the end and you've gone to Hell, it shakes you up. It makes you reevaluate everything about your life, accomplishments, purpose, etc. If you are blessed enough to emerge from an experience like this, you are not the same person you were when you went in.

Funny, but not everybody likes the person who comes out—preferring instead the person who went in. But more about this important observation in subsequent chapters.

All this spun through my consciousness as I plunged into unimaginable depths of "burning" and scintillating cold, darkness, despair, and emptiness.

Like a whisper of smoke, I was this disembodied entity, slowly being sucked downward into this blackness that got colder and more terrifying and indescribably dark, total isolation from anything comforting, good or loving.

It was/is as real as the sun or the tides or the feeling of gravity. Still, I struggled to find and move towards Claudia's voice.

One of the worst, most nightmarish parts of this whole experience is that I even imagined my own funeral. This included the moment that my body was lowered into the ground and everyone walked away from the gravesite as darkness fell.

I could hear my friends and family giving eulogies in the chapel prior to my burial at Forest Lawn Memorial Park. As my wife, mother, sons, and others expressed their grief over losing me, some read from prepared notes, while others spoke directly from the heart, struggling to speak through their tears.

Others prepared pre-recorded videos that they had made for this occasion. (Honestly, some of them could've done better than making statements such as, "...if only I had five more minutes with him . . . ")

As I envisioned my loved ones eulogizing me, it was almost as if, for some of them, their skin was a different tint, like they were not quite human or they were some other type of being. This was as terrifying and troubling as anything else in this nightmare that felt like a terrible train ride.

Literally, because I felt myself laying there in a beautiful coffin while riding in the back of the hearse on the way to Forest Lawn. I even imagined from the sequence of turns exactly where we were on Riverside, or Barham, etc. on our way to the gravesite at Forest Lawn in Hollywood Hills. That's where the rest of my family from the United States is buried.

My coffin was visually attractive, but inside it was cold and dark, rock hard and uncomfortable. The thin padding—which was only a few centimeters deep—may have looked plush and cozy, but it was not.

Then at the cemetery, I could also feel my body shifting as my weary family carried the heavy coffin from the hearse to the grave. There I could smell the freshly dug dirt and the aromatic flowers that were laid out on mounds of earth around the hole where I would be buried. At the same time, I felt like I was already in that grave.

My near-death nightmare inspired me and Claudia to purchase above-ground "companion" crypts—which hold two coffins in one crypt—so that my gravesite vision can never happen.

Awakening to a Living Nightmare

After I awakened from that near cardiac death experience, my sons arrived from Florida, just as a Catholic priest (out of pure coincidence) was visiting me and giving me last rites "just in case."

The "frosting on the cake" was what happened immediately after that. The Critical Care Pulmonologist walked in and casually asked me: "So, what did you see while you were gone?"

I would learn later that Claudia had to trick or fight her way into my ICU room against the regulations and protocols of hospital security. Our family had reportedly been told to go sit somewhere in a room and just wait, but no one could stop Claudia from getting to and staying at my bedside.

If she hadn't fought against all authority, against all odds, I would never have heard her voice calling—more like demanding—that I return from death.

Which I miraculously did.

This "return" occurred over an agonizing period of time.

It was one Hell of a fight, as God permitted her to pray and heard her prayers, so strong was and is her faith. Neither my faith, nor will, are as strong as hers, and I would not have made it across that bridge back to life if it were not for her strength.

Little did we realize at the time, but we were about

to begin to go through a nearly ten-year struggle for life; we liken the emotional, financial, physical, and spiritually mind-bending experiences to being in a meat grinder. Those years were so grim, that we wondered if I had been cursed. Unfortunately, I am still considering the possibility of a curse.

However, I later realized that there may be an alternate and valid explanation as well.

I would like to offer the sausage that came out of that "meat grinder" as a gift to you.

If you've read Deuteronomy in the Bible, you'll find what I found, which is that I met all of the criteria, or in other words checked all the boxes, to describe someone who has been cursed. Specifically, the descriptions of health-related curses as a punishment for wrongs that I have committed in my life.

The criteria for being cursed are basically disobedience to God's Commandments as laid out in Deuteronomy 28—which details the blessings for following God's Commandments and punishments for disobedience.

I will be the first to admit that you have to be pretty desperate to start looking at Deuteronomy and curses to try and understand what's happening to you.

When I finish telling you the unbelievable combination of medical disasters that happened to me during those ten years leading up to the heart transplant, you will understand. For now, I'm sticking primarily with the cardiac issues, because those were the most acute, urgent, and relentless in trying to finish me off during this period of time.

It is worth noting, however, that during this entire time, I also battled prostate cancer, multiple hip fractures, acute gallstone pancreatitis that required emergency surgical removal, and a spinal tumor that left me partially paralyzed and plagued by chronic pain. But those are serious, life-threatening stories for another day. All of which Claudia had to suffer through and endure along with me.

I will conclude this chapter by stating that it would've been much easier to keep sinking back into the darkness, terrifying and nightmarish as it was, than push through the physical pain of returning to life.

Yet I had to push through the pain of broken ribs from CPR. I had chest pain from the actual heart attack and blocked heart vessels and damaged teeth from the intubation. Worst of all was the struggle against the ventilator, which felt like I was choking, drowning, and suffocating all at the same time.

All this, while simultaneously struggling with the realization that I would be dead were it not for Claudia and total life support.

I, unlike certain hollow eulogies, actually would walk through fire to live ten more minutes with Claudia. And during my ten-year health crisis, I pretty much found myself doing exactly that over and over.

Hauntingly and unforgettably, there was a definite, malevolent force, like some kind of opioid being sprayed on me each NDE episode, to make me want to stop fighting, and just sink back into that hole of horrible darkness for infinity.

Little did I know, nine more of these awful adventures awaited me. They started to eerily echo the lyrics of that Paul Simon song, "Hello Darkness, My Old Friend."

My beautiful wife Claudia is so full of life and literally saved mine.

Chapter 2

Fighting for My Husband's Life and Love

By Claudia Treuherz

To understand me better, I have to take you for a quick tour into my childhood. I was born and grew up in Romania. Romania is predominantly Orthodox, yet my family was a mixture of Baptist Christians and Pentecostal Christians. However, Christianity was illegal under the communist government, so attending church inspired a feeling of defiance, power, and a little fear.

Thankfully, my family moved to the United States after my father was able to defect (which meant rejecting the political system of Romania at that time). Because Romania was a communist country, he was granted asylum.

Therefore, my mother, my sister, and I were able to leave Romania, but not without a fight. After two years of waiting, our visas were granted. We finally arrived in the USA about two and a half years after my father.

At the time, I was fourteen and a half years old. This experience filled me with happiness, excitement, and pride. The land of the brave and the home of the free, as *The Star-Spangled Banner* says, became our new home.

I can tell you with certainty that seeing a grocery store in the United States for the first time blew my mind. I couldn't believe the quantity, the quality, the variety, and availability of so much food. In a communist country, food is scarce, and lines are long. There are rations determined by the number of family members, and there was absolutely no variety of anything.

I remember trying peanut butter for the first time. Oh, my God, I was hooked, not to mention my first sip of Sprite and a slice of pizza. I thought that was the most amazing food I had ever tasted in my life.

I always looked forward to getting a slice of pizza after school. It was only 25 cents and my dad gave me a jar filled with quarters. There were a lot of future slices in that jar.

It was amazing that we no longer had to wait in line for bread or milk, or anything else for that matter. My life had just been upgraded. Not only did I experience an abundance of food, but I also finally felt free and unafraid.

Not that it was easy; it was not. I did not speak English, and I was an awkward teenager whose parents made me wear short haircuts with no make-up, no short skirts, or anything revealing. I was never allowed to have a sleepover or attend one. Making friends was not easy. We moved all the time. I attended five different high schools.

Throughout high school, I was bullied for being a foreigner, and for having an accent.

"Commie!" a jock taunted.

I distinctly remember that moment, which prompted all the other kids to join in and call me that for a long time. Most of them couldn't find Romania on the map. Why would I be bothered by kids who had no clue where I had come from? Yet, I *was* bothered. I wanted to fit in. My family had escaped communism, but here I was being bullied for being a communist. I was crushed and confused. I did not understand racism.

In my country of birth, there was no such thing as racism. This was a new concept. It only motivated me to learn English, and to try really hard to shed my accent and blend in. Failure was not an option. That same tenacity would come in handy all throughout my life.

My faith and belief in Jesus Christ were a gift that I was privileged to receive through my amazing maternal grandfather. His strong faith and godliness made an impact on my later life. Even today, I hear his teachings.

Yes, I learned about God, and believed in God, yet I was anything but a good Christian. Unfortunately, I was what would be considered a lukewarm Christian for many years. I will go so far to call myself a hypocrite. I prayed when I needed something and instantly forgot God the moment things got good. Although I attended church most Sundays at various times throughout my life, I was a fraud. Neither here nor there.

It's a good thing God has infinite mercy and patience— something I was never good at. Patience, that is. Despite my poor faith, God challenged me over and over, forcing me to face Him.

When October 29, 2015, hit, I felt as if I was on the battlefield, the enemy was closing in, surrounding me, and the firing squad was ready to aim and shoot. If I had not had God in my life and my faith, I do not believe I could have weathered the storm that laid ahead.

"Poor faith" sounds like a contradiction, yet I couldn't have done without it. I guess it *is* a contradiction. Faith deepens with time, circumstances, influences, and experiences.

My parents were considered "normal" in eastern European circles. Let's just say, they did not spare the rod. I will not write about the woes of my childhood; however, I will briefly share how they shaped me as a human being, mother, and wife.

The choice was simple—repeat history or break the chains of my ancestors and become the opposite of what I was destined to become. History really does not repeat itself; people repeat history.

I chose to be different. I had the power to choose. I was not a victim; I was a victor. I never took NO for an answer. I fought for what I believed in, worked hard for what I had, and faked it till I made it when necessary.

That said, I still managed to marry poorly the first time and make some additional bad decisions along the way. However, I created two amazing children.

Looking back, I would probably change nothing. Regret only means that I did not learn anything of value from my mistakes. You can always find something good and beautiful, even in the worst of circumstances, and God knows I've had quite a few terrible circumstances.

Every storm ends. However, my experience has shown that rarely does life allow us any length of time in between crises.

I learned quite early on that I needed to look at people's good qualities rather than their shortcomings. Everybody has both. It is just a matter of choice which side you want to see. That taught me that if I focus on the positive, rather than the negative, I can overcome quite a lot.

It is so much easier to dwell on the negative; somehow, it's effortless. Staying positive takes discipline and faith.

As I learned that everybody has two or more sides to them, diplomacy became an art for me. And instead of conflict, I search for resolution. It took some time to polish it and make it work, but that is the beauty of time; it allows for the opportunity of constant learning and evolving.

I am not the same person I was ten years ago. Back then, I was not the same person I was ten years before that. Change is inevitable.

How we change is a choice.

Being in a bad marriage does not have to mean "lost time" or "lost youth." I view it as, "I have learned what not to do, what not to say." I learned how impactful words, as well as the lack of words and actions, can shape and construct reality.

Why am I telling you all this? To give you a backdrop of what's to come.

Ten 2nd Chances

I wonder how many people can say, "I saw my husband die TEN times."

When I met Robert, I knew I had met my forever. He was to me, the shade and the oasis you find while wandering alone through a hot scorching desert. If I were a dandelion, he was the wind beneath my fluff. He was that cold drink of water on a hot sunny day.

Our love felt so intense, yet so familiar and intimate from day one. I felt as if we had already been together for 1,000 years and we were just picking up where we had left off. I do not believe in past lives, but it certainly felt as if we had lived many lifetimes together.

Our bond was undeniable and unbreakable, even by death. I truly mean that in every sense of the word—death. Our marriage was the epitome of happiness, love, success, and joy. We were that cliché postcard image of two lovers, in eternal bliss, or so we thought.

Life is not always fair, and I never expected it to be. I just didn't think it could get so derailed, so hard and soul wrenching.

When the obstacles started to align in our path, there was no light at the end of our tunnel. We were in the dark for a very long time. However, we never lost faith; we never lost hope.

Throughout the years, it felt as if we were both hurtling towards a light that was so dim, so far away, so unreachable, yet we were both determined to somehow reach it. I told myself daily, "You'll get there."

As long as Rob was by my side, I didn't care how bumpy the road got. We were going to get through it. Bumps in the road, we got in abundance.

On October 29th, 2015, Rob and I had a horrific car accident that changed the direction of our lives 180 degrees. The accident precipitated a heart attack for Rob. His heart deteriorated in the course of two weeks due to medical negligence and/or lack of medical intervention. It profoundly changed both of us physically, mentally, and spiritually.

However, it did not change the love we had for each other. Watching him die, watching him get defibrillated, seeing him on life support, is not something I will ever forget or get over. Going back in my mind nine years ago to the dreadful day when he coded, brings back emotions that I still struggle with today.

The head-on collision was so violent, so intense, that my brain keeps trying to shut out those memories to protect my sanity. The impact was so powerful, it left me in a state of confusion. I had only realized that we had been in an accident after I saw the broken windshield. I was confused as to why the car was filling with smoke, my brain was foggy, my neurons were not firing.

Once the fog lifted, I felt a searing pain in my neck, my chest, and my shoulder. The pain was debilitating. I was screaming from the pain. I did not want to scream or cry, yet my brain was not listening. The moans and screams kept coming. I did not recognize my own voice; it was as if it were somebody else moaning and crying. I felt so powerless to the pain. The pain was winning and I was losing.

Fortunately, an ambulance was at the intersection at the time of impact.

I remember being taken out of the car; I was screaming and then suddenly, I was in an ambulance. It felt as if I was losing time because everything seemed surreal.

Fear gripped my whole being. I did not know if Rob

was okay. The ambulance personnel assumed I was more hurt, therefore I was triaged and taken to the hospital first. I was strapped to the gurney, unable to move.

As I was waiting in the hospital hallway to be seen by a doctor, I saw through the corner of my eye that another gurney was passing by. On it, I saw an arm and Rob's watch.

I immediately knew it was him on that gurney.

"Rob!" I screamed.

All I got in return was a faint "I love you," as they wheeled him away.

My screams dispatched a nurse who casually told me, "Your husband had a heart attack. They are taking him to the Cath Lab." She quickly disappeared, leaving me with my thoughts. They quickly turned gloomy as I was literally left in the dark with information I could barely process.

In my desperation to gain some sort of control and to find some information about Rob, I demanded, "Somebody please remove these restraints!"

Nobody listened; nobody came to remove the restraints.

"It's for your own protection," they said, "to limit the injury you sustained."

I was sinking deeper and deeper into the abyss of desperation.

Many hours later, I was told that my husband had a stent inserted into his "LAD" (Left Anterior Descending

Artery). That was so foreign to me; I had very little knowledge about heart disease, even less what the LAD was.

I knew instantly that I would be navigating through uncharted territory. I was not prepared. I was not ready. I was scared. Terrified. Nobody would sign up for this. I most certainly never expected this calamity, but here I was, facing it and being put in the hot seat to deal with it.

I finally got to see Rob *three days later*. I was wheeled into his room by an orderly, while a nurse awaited my arrival. I studied her face, and I knew she was going to give me bad news.

Rob looked gray like he was dying. Fear occupied my mind, and my body wouldn't cooperate. I couldn't stand up or walk out of the wheelchair; I was locked in place by self-induced paralysis. Again, why was my brain so weak? What was happening to me? I had thought I was strong.

The nurse wasted no time, automatically launching into a tirade about how sick Rob was, attempting to encapsulate heart disease in her speech. Clearly, she realized I knew nothing about heart disease or what was to come.

"His ejection fraction is between 11 and 13," she said.

I had no idea what it meant.

"Will he survive?" I asked.

Her cold comment still lingers in my mind: "I don't know, I don't know. All I can tell you is that your life is about to change and not for the better."

Anger rose and coursed through my veins. Her cold, chilling words were heartless. At that moment I said, "You don't know us lady! We will overcome this."

She literally scoffed and walked out, giving us a moment of privacy. I kissed Rob gently, I whispered many I love you's in his ear, and told him with absolute authority, "This too shall pass, and you will get better. I am not losing you." Then they rolled me back to my room.

After I was discharged, I was fortunate to have good friends who helped in my recovery and drove me to the hospital daily to see Robert. For two weeks, I watched Rob's health deteriorate further and further as he was begging me to get him out of that hospital. He kept saying, "They are letting me die."

A week after he was admitted at a different hospital and was awaiting another angiogram, I sat in a large waiting room that felt like the walls were closing in.

As I was waiting for the doctor to come and give me any news, I braced myself, feeling that the news would not be good. The doctor's first words were, "He's a very sick man. I don't know how he survived all this time."

He explained that the first stent he had received at the first hospital had failed. Apparently, it was undersized and/or under expanded, therefore blocking the LAD—the Left Anterior Descending Artery—which supplies blood to the left ventricle. This is the chamber of the heart responsible for pushing blood out of the heart and to the rest of the body. So damage here can be catastrophic.

It had failed immediately, causing permanent damage to his heart. It was hard to believe that very well-trained physicians in a Level 1 Trauma Center would allow this to happen, but it did. The doctor said that he had just fixed the stent and inserted another in a different artery. The prognosis was grim, but Rob was alive, for now.

He was given an angiogram, which is an X-ray of blood vessels and blood flow, and it helps doctors diagnose and observe cardiovascular conditions. An angiogram is normally an outpatient procedure, but given his condition, they felt it would be better to keep him in the hospital for observations. So Rob was moved to the Telemetry floor, a special unit where his heart rhythm and vital signs were carefully monitored.

A day and night passed with no complications or incidents. I decided to make a quick run home to shower and pick up lunch. I had already driven the nurses crazy with concerns about his low blood pressure. Everyone assured me that his low blood pressure was okay. The eerie feeling, however, did not escape my mind. Despite it, I shook it off and went home to shower.

I called him constantly just to hear his voice. We were having a casual conversation when suddenly, he stopped talking mid-sentence. All I could hear was commotion in the background.

The call ended abruptly with no explanation. I called him back, but nobody answered. A few minutes later, I received a call from my mother-in-law.

"Please come back to the hospital," she said with no explanation.

Deep down in my soul, I knew something terrible had occurred.

I called the hospital and asked to speak with Rob's nurse.

"Are you driving?" the nurse asked nonchalantly.

"Yes."

"We'll talk when you get back here," he said.

It was a dead giveaway of how bad the situation was. At that moment, I knew that Rob had coded. I ran every red light, drove over many curbs, and sped through wrong-way areas to avoid traffic and get back to the hospital.

I drove like a lunatic and was surprised I did not get pulled over. I don't even know how I made it back to the hospital without incident. I do not recommend anybody doing that. I was reckless and was not thinking clearly.

My in-laws were in the lobby waiting for me, a bad sign. Although I already knew he had coded, hearing it from my mother-in-law seemed to have solidified my nightmare. I literally fell to my knees and wailed. I was inconsolable.

My father-in-law helped me off the floor and tried to guide me into a sitting area where we were supposed to wait for a grief counselor and security officer to arrive.

"You're not allowed to go in the Intensive Care Unit to see him," they told me.

I snapped. I had to get in there. It was urgent. I had to fight for him and with him. I rang the bell of the unit and waited. A voice came over the speaker.

"I'm here to see my husband," I said calmly.

I got buzzed in without questions about who my husband was. I had no idea where he was, as this was not the Telemetry floor where I had left him. I ran throughout the Intensive Care Unit, looking from room to room until I found him.

Intubated. Eyes halfway open, looking dead. My Rob was not in there. The man lying in that bed was hollow, not present, not dead, yet not alive. Medical personnel were all around him, feverishly working to keep him alive.

Seeing him on Life Support was surreal. His eyes were partially open, but there was no life in them. His beautiful green eyes were gray and flat. The systematic breathing machine was the only thing I could hear as I was right outside the glass room in the ICU. It sounded so clinical, so far removed from life. His body was limp. His face looked almost deformed as the breathing tube was tugging the side of his face. I couldn't believe this was my vibrant, full of life and full of love husband. I was shouting in my mind, *Father God, please don't take him yet, please, please, please!*

When someone motioned that it was safe for me to enter, I walked in. My heart sank. I felt overwhelmed by sadness and fear of losing him. At that moment, I felt a tug at my heart that said, *pray.* I kneeled at his head and started praying. After a while, the room seemed to get very quiet.

"He's most likely gone," a nurse was trying to explain. "The machines are keeping him alive. Are there other family members who need to be contacted? A social worker might be helpful."

I couldn't comprehend why I would need a social worker.

She performed a few neurological tests for my benefit. They showed no sign of brain activity, since he did not respond to painful stimuli.

"Do you understand what I'm trying to say?" she asked repeatedly, as if I were deaf.

Of course I understood. I was just not going to accept what she was telling me. I did not give up hope. I did not want to fall into despair. I had faith he would make it.

Eventually, all medical personnel left the room, leaving me and my in-laws alone to "absorb" the situation. I continued to pray, holding his hand and stroking his face, talking to him.

"Come back to me, come back to me," I said repeatedly.

I felt him squeeze my hand, or I thought I did. I wanted to believe he was squeezing my hand.

"That was an involuntary jerk," a nurse said, "caused by muscles randomly contracting."

"No," I told her. I was willing to believe my words to be true; I felt that he was trying to communicate with me. He continued to randomly squeeze my hand throughout the night.

"Don't make me come in there to get you!" I threatened. "Please come back to me."

Keep in mind, I was told he most likely could not hear me. I believe that our love was that invisible tether line that kept pulling, pushing, tugging, and prompting him to return. I believed that he could hear me.

I felt him wanting to live, wanting to come back, but that he couldn't find his way. It was as if our souls were tangled together and unwilling to let go of each other. I was not going to let go. I prayed harder.

I felt that I needed to guide him. I felt him calling out to me as I was deep in prayer. I called out to him over and over. In the darkness, he heard me calling him back, pleading and begging him not to leave me all alone.

Incredibly, after he "came back," he repeated word for word what I had said to him. After a while, he told me how he "swam" back to me through pure evil darkness.

He swam towards my voice, as if my voice were the piety rope he was reaching for. The closer he got to my voice, he said, the harder it got to move forward.

I would later learn that the evil darkness did not want to relinquish him. And that the pain he was experiencing as he was approaching my voice was excruciating and it would have been easier to let go, but he didn't; he fought.

He did not want to go back into that gelatin of evil and dark nothingness. He bravely moved forward until he felt my hand, saw my eyes and extended his hand to touch my face to see if I were real. He seemed confused, as if unsure if he were dead or alive.

It was not an easy return for him. Since they did not expect him to wake up, they did not administer any sedatives, or paralytic drugs, as they do for most people who are intubated.

When he fully opened his eyes and realized what was happening, I saw the sheer terror and panic in his eyes. I felt that he indeed had traveled from a place of darkness that only Anubis, the ancient Egyptian god of the dead, would be comfortable with.

It was very late at night and the nurse he was assigned to in the ICU was a floater from another floor. She did not belong in the ICU. I guess everybody assumed he was a goner and therefore would not require much medical attention.

They were wrong.

As he came to, the nurse was useless. I think she was more scared than I was.

"Get a doctor!" I screamed as she literally ran and hid in the stairwell. "Get a doctor! Get a doctor!"

My screams and banging on the nurses' station most definitely attracted the attention of other medical personnel.

My hysterical behavior mortified my in-laws, who are very proper.

I didn't care. I ran back into Rob's room. He was trying to pull the intubation tube from his throat. I held him down. His parents, who are older, could not restrain him.

He was choking and gagging, desperate to remove the tube from his throat. He was turning purple, and my heart was racing like a NASCAR vehicle.

When a person is intubated, a machine does the breathing for them. Waking up intubated gives them a choking sensation.

I was desperate for help and terrified he would code again from stress. I even called his internal medicine physician on his cell phone, since he was the chief of staff at the hospital, begging him to put in orders to remove the intubation.

But nothing happens fast in a hospital.

Meanwhile, Rob was choking and struggling to breathe through the intubation. The key was to match his breathing to the machine, so I tried to demonstrate.

"Breath simultaneously with me," I said as I matched my own breathing to the cadence of the machine.

Watching me and trying to synchronize his breathing pattern to the ventilator's rate seemed to calm him a little. He was allowing the ventilator to do the breathing for him; it was not easy, and it did not last long. We still needed help. Urgently.

"Take the tube out!" I screamed as his cardiologist ran down the hallway towards his room.

Finally, the respiratory physician approached. She did the sign of the cross on her chest and said, "In the last sixteen years, I have never seen this."

"I'm glad we made history," I said, "but get the damn tube out!"

She did.

When Rob was able to talk, his first words were, "I am back." His voice was coarse, and he sounded scared. He kept repeating, "I went to a very dark place, but I heard your voice calling me back."

Those words, and his terrifying description of what happened and where he "went," still haunt me today.

"I believe I went to Hell," he said.

The way I understood it, was that he went to a place that was completely separated from the divine. There was no shred or even a smear of love, only hatred, fear, and loneliness. He said that his words failed to fully describe what he saw and what he felt.

Paradoxically, I can only imagine how incredible Heaven would have been in contrast to Hell. I'm pretty certain words would also fail to describe Heaven.

I wish that hearing the words "I'm back" had been the last time I would hear them. Oh no, I would hear them nine more times throughout the next nine years. Because the beginning of our journey through the valley of death was just starting.

To relive in granular detail the hardships that followed and could expand this chapter into a whole book; therefore, I will narrow it down.

Little did I know that I would become an expert on cardiac medical terms, tests, and procedures. For example, the ejection fraction (EF) is a measurement, expressed as a percentage, of how much blood the left ventricle pumps out with each contraction. It's an important indicator of how well your heart is functioning. A normal ejection fraction is typically between fifty percent and seventy percent. As Rob's heart function decreased, his EF was measured at less than fifteen percent. A heart with a fifteen percent EF is barely compatible with sustaining life. In addition to functioning poorly as a pump, a weakened heart muscle is also more prone to electrical instability. This can trigger abnormal heart rhythms such as ventricular tachycardia (V-tach) and ventricular fibrillation (V-fib).

For this reason, the doctors decided to implant a pacemaker/defibrillator in his chest, under the skin. This device delivers electrical shocks to restore the heart to a normal rhythm. It works by sending small electrical impulses to "pace" the heart. It also monitors for dangerous abnormal heart rhythms, called arrhythmias. If one is detected, the defibrillator releases a powerful shock to correct the arrhythmia and return the heart to a normal healthy rhythm.

Thank heavens the doctors did this procedure, because I have watched Rob go into V-tach/V-fib nine more times over the years. Each V-tach/V-fib episode was terrifying. His face changed; it contorted into a death mask, and he just dropped. The defibrillator took a few seconds to shock him. After he received the shocks, it took a little time for him to get his bearings. The heart got restarted, but the brain needed a little time to catch up. Watching somebody get shocked is violent.

If he coughed funny or if he breathed in the way I deemed different or weird, fear overwhelmed me, and my heart immediately started racing. I was not surprised to find out that I developed arrhythmia issues that eventually needed an ablation. (This medical procedure treats irregular heart rhythms. It involves creating small scars in the heart tissue to block abnormal electrical signals that cause these arrhythmias. This is typically done using thin, flexible tubes called catheters, which are guided through blood vessels to the heart. The procedure uses heat in the form of radiofrequency energy or cold, which is called cryoablation to create the scars.) I called my arrhythmia "Broken Heart Syndrome." Talk about having some serious PTSD.

To add to my Post Traumatic Stress Disorder, we had a major snow blizzard in 2022. Snowfall in some areas was more than fifteen feet, with snow drifts over twenty feet. We were completely snowed in with no possibility of getting out or getting help in case of a medical emergency. Having watched Robert go into V-tach many times, I was ridden with anxiety, thinking, *what if it happens while nobody could get to us?*

Although I knew in my heart that God was watching over us, my brain was still reacting to the blizzard conditions. I am human, I am not perfect, and I still allow anxiety to creep in, despite my deep faith. That said, let me regress and go back to the earlier stages of our drawn-out nightmare.

We went from very serious cardiac issues with multiple episodes of sudden cardiac death, to a garden variety of other very serious health crises unrelated to the heart. They started with a left hip fracture that required total hip replacement, followed by another cardiac arrest, acute pancreatitis and cholecystitis, prostate cancer followed by radiation, more cardiac arrest in between, a right hip fracture requiring another total hip replacement, a massive spinal tumor that left him partially paralyzed on the right-side post-surgery, and the finale was the heart transplant. All in the span of nine years. It almost sounds made up or like a scary movie filled with health-related nightmares and curses, yet it's all true.

The spinal tumor was a catastrophic development. I was the first to find out about it and the weight of it was crushing. After learning about the tumor, I had to drive about ninety miles to get home from the hospital. All I remember about that drive is crying and shouting out to God. I was crying tears of sorrow with heart-wrenching sadness. Once again, our world had suffered another earth-shaking blow. I wondered, *how many blows can we still take and not lose the fight?* I couldn't answer the question at that time. I was spent.

We were given some hope that the removal of the tumor was a routine and somewhat easy procedure, and that Rob would have no long-term damage. That news was like a breath of fresh air. The first surgery would repair the broken hip with a total hip replacement and the second surgery would remove the spinal tumor. Two back-to-back surgeries, only days apart. My nerves were fried; I was exhausted and frazzled. The spinal tumor surgery finally happened. It went without any incident, so I was told.

However, I noticed that his right arm was completely paralyzed after waking up from surgery.

"Function will return within a few hours or potentially a few days," the medical staff told us.

Days came and went, yet the right arm and right leg remained paralyzed. After a few weeks, the neurosurgeon told us that sometimes the spinal cord needs a little more time to start functioning properly after a surgery. We were still hopeful, especially since he said, "It would be unethical of me to tell you that you'll regain function, if I didn't think it would happen."

Well, more than a year has passed, and Rob's right hand is still partially paralyzed, and his right leg is very weak.

Once again, we found out the hard way that not every surgeon is equal in skills. This neurosurgeon did a very bad job, and I could say with absolute clarity that he is responsible for paralyzing my husband. Some people might ask what I base this opinion on. It's simple—a post-op MRI done in preparation for the heart transplant conclusively demonstrated post-surgical spinal damage, with formation of fibrous tissue around the surrounding structures of the spinal cord (annular scarring).

I had to watch Robert learn to walk again, feed himself, dress himself, bathe himself, and write with his left hand, although he is right-handed. He no longer could drive or do any physical activities without excruciating pain. He now lives in pain all the time, yet his joy for life and love for me and our children remains eternal. He powers through it and cries when he thinks I don't see him. He is my rock as much as I am his.

You might ask, *how can one person go through so many health crises and still be alive?* Believe me, I asked myself the same question. The spinal tumor, although a very bad diagnosis, was not the BIG finale. The heart transplant that happened less than six months later after the spinal tumor, was the grand finale, the coronation.

Our lives did turn into a tug of war with sickness and death; however, we were in it to win it, so giving up was not an option or a thought. At times I felt that we were navigating through a dark storm. Sickness and death were pulling at us, and we pulled back harder. We were ready to dance in the storm, face the winds, battle the cold and reach the sunrise. After close to a decade, we came out victorious.

Our foundation is built on rock, not sand, and we remained standing through it all. The storm, the deluge, revealed how strong our foundation really was. My faith in time became very strong; it was unwavering, fierce, and unmovable. Every day it gets stronger.

Each morning when I wake up and feel Robert next to me, breathing, alive, I thank God and pray for a blessed day. I know evil is only inches away, lurking, ready to pounce.

I never believed in curses, but I'm here to tell you that they do exist. They are real and terrifying. The antidote to curses can only be love, prayer, and asking for forgiveness for whatever one has done to be cursed.

Or maybe it was just negative and evil wishes of others that follow us like a shadow. Whatever the case, I prayed that God would liberate us and send all the evil back to its original source or into the depths of Hell. God heard my cries and answered. Prayer was my refuge.

We live in a turbulent world, where up is down, and down is up, but the one thing constant and real and wholesome is the love Rob and I have for each other and for our children.

Everyone in this world carries some form of baggage, filled with loathing, pettiness, preconceived notions, hurt, and worthlessness. We fill that baggage over time. We accumulate insults from decades ago, hard feelings, ill feelings, and hatred. Some people are unable or unwilling to empty that baggage.

Small-minded people hold on to those feelings all throughout their lives, taking all that negativity with them into death. It's like drinking poison but expecting somebody else to die.

I guess some people forget the good, but they sure remember in granular detail the perceived infraction that was inflicted upon them. Those kinds of people are unable to evolve, therefore, they live in the past with all the demons torturing them, never achieving happiness.

After Rob coded and came back to life, he had changed one hundred percent. The past was gone; forgiveness and redemption were the main focus of his life. He forgave others who had wronged him and most importantly, he forgave himself for what he perceived to have done wrong.

He became a better person for me, for our children, and for himself. Our love deepened even more throughout the most challenging ten years of our lives. It united us and bonded us together; we were forged.

We lived with the dark cloud above us, following us for those nine years. From the time of the accident and heart attack to the heart transplant, it was exactly 432 weeks. Not a day over or under it.

Angel number 432 (in numerology, an angel number is believed to be a message or sign from angels, offering guidance and confirmation) holds profound significance and serves as a beacon of light on our spiritual path. It's a reminder that we are never alone, and that the universe is conspiring in our favor, with God's will.

Oh boy, that proved to be more true than you could possibly imagine.

We started with a near-fatal car crash and a massive heart attack on Thursday, October 29, 2015, and ended with the heart transplant on Thursday, February 15, 2024—exactly 432 weeks later. Talk about divine intervention at the exact proper moment.

The journey to the heart transplant was long and riddled with obstacles. I would like to take a moment and tell you the immediate events that led to the transplant.

On January 2, 2024, after spending a beautiful Christmas with our children and grandchildren in Florida, I heard a big thump behind me. My Robert had collapsed and was laying on the floor.

I immediately knew the shock from his defibrillator was coming next. I watched him go limp. His eyes were rolling back in his head. His face contorted. His chest raised as the defibrillator did its job and shocked him.

I thought I was screaming . . . I was. I was terrified. No intelligible words were coming out of my mouth, only blabber. My daughter called 911.

"Without a heart transplant," the doctors told us at the hospital, "he will not survive much longer."

He had already been accepted for a heart transplant by UCLA in 2017, but because of the drastic cardiac reversal program that he had entered, he was able to buy himself nine more years of life with the "old" heart.

But now time was definitely up.

He had reached the end, and things were falling apart quickly. All they could do for him at this hospital in Florida was to give him more and more amiodarone (a medication with horrible side effects that is used to treat life-threatening heart rhythm disorders) and allow him to continue getting shocked over and over again, until eventually, the defibrillator would fail. We had to find a way to get back to Los Angeles and go to UCLA.

UCLA's heart transplant program is known for its excellent patient outcomes, with graft survival rates and transplant patient survival rates exceeding national averages.[6] According to the Scientific Registry for Transplant Recipients (SRTR), the UCLA program has the lowest donor-heart rejection and highest survival rate in the country, at just five percent rejection compared to the national average of twenty-five percent.[7]

Getting back to Los Angeles from Florida was nothing short of a miracle.

The Florida hospital would not discharge Rob to fly commercial; they would only approve a flight on an air ambulance. I attempted to get three air ambulance

[6] "Patient Survival Rates," UCLA Health, accessed May 4, 2025, https://www.uclahealth.org/medical-services/transplants/about-us/patient-survival-rates.

[7] Scientific Registry of Transplant Recipients, *Program-Specific Report: University of California at Los Angeles Medical Center, Heart Transplant Program*, released January 7, 2025, based on data available as of October 31, 2024, accessed May 4, 2025, https://www.srtr.org/PDFs/012025_release/pdfPSR/CAUCTX1HR202411PNEW.pdf.

flights, but all fell through. Coordinating between two hospitals, navigating through red tape, bed control, and the air ambulance company was impossible.

Days were passing and they couldn't get it together. I had to take matters into my own hands and get us home. So, I booked two tickets on JetBlue business class.

We had to sign out against medical advice (AMA) at 5:00 a.m. to catch the flight from Fort Lauderdale to Los Angeles. Thank heavens the airline was running on time. Except, something was wrong with the airplane door. The flight was almost cancelled. The flight attendant was aware of our situation (I had told her that my husband was very ill, and we were flying back for a heart transplant). The flight attendant informed the captain, who made calls and insisted on having the door fixed. By the grace of God, the airplane door was fixed and we took off. I will always be grateful to the flight attendant and the captain on our JetBlue flight.

Still, the flight was terrifying. It was draining to know that Rob could go into V-tach at any moment and there would be nothing anybody could do to help.

We took a major chance, but it paid off. We landed without incident, then drove directly to UCLA. We were on the road to a transplant.

Through it all, Robert and I never lost hope, never became depressed, and we certainly never gave up. Rob was always strong and positive. His upbeat outlook on life sustained me through the darkest of days.

After being on the UNOS—the United Network for Organ Donation—for only three weeks, we got the call. It was Valentine's Day 2024, late in the day. We were told there is a perfect match. A gift of a heart on Valentine's Day. Does it get any better? Can there be a more precious gift?

The transplant was scheduled for 5:00 a.m. the next day. Imagine waiting for updates on how the surgery is progressing. It's like sitting on pins and needles. Uncanny.

The communication from the OR was all through text. I was pacing for hours. Finally, I got the last text: *Surgery complete. Patient moved to Recovery.*

I got to see him later that day. He was still intubated and unconscious.

"He's fighting," the medical staff told me. "Expect anything."

Nurse Jackie warned, "He's very sick. Be cautiously optimistic, because things were not quite right with the heart."

Apparently, it had come all the way from Dallas, Texas. It had traveled for a while to get to Los Angeles. Being on ice for such a long time, although it was within the maximum allowed time a heart could survive outside of the body, it had struggled to get going.

The heart was stunned. As it happens, it was transported in the latest, most modern technology available for transfer of a living, suspended organ.

The surgeon would tell us later that it was transported in what was called a SherpaPak—a very sophisticated device that would diffuse fluid, electrolytes, heat, and cold across tissue as needed to sustain it as long as possible.

I learned that after they had transplanted the heart into Robert's chest, the surgeon had had to leave the chest open while manually massaging the heart for one and a half hours before it would start. All while keeping him on the bypass machine. That scary thought filled me with dread.

Once again, I was faced with the same words: "He's very sick; be cautiously optimistic." My heart sank, no pun intended.

At one point they told me, "We're going to wake him to see if he'll breathe on his own." They also wanted to see if he would respond to whatever other tests they were going to perform on him.

It was another terrifying experience once again. Not knowing if he would wake up or be able to breathe on his own was very disconcerting. I didn't know what to expect.

He slowly woke up and realized he was intubated. The look of horror on his face was too much to bear. He desperately tried to communicate with me through hand gestures. I knew he was scared.

"Please put him under again," I asked the nurse.

"We're already administering the necessary medications to do that," she said, "but it's a slow process on purpose, so as to not allow his BP to crash."

At least I knew he could wake up. I do not know how I did not lose my mind. I was very close to breaking down. Through God's grace, we made it through.

The ventilator was removed a day later. His journey to recovery was just beginning. We all have watched shows that depict a transplant operation as the end of dying and smooth sailing afterwards. I wish it had been like that. The actual heart transplant procedure is just the beginning.

Afterwards is when the work begins. There were weekly biopsies, handfuls of medications that needed to be carefully monitored with weekly bloodwork. The meds also required constant adjustments in dose, weekly or sometimes biweekly clinic visits, echocardiograms, weekly COVID-19 tests, rejection treatment that required hospitalizations, etc.

It is an exhausting process that cannot possibly be done without a committed and devoted family member. You must be willing to put yourself last. Otherwise, it is impossible to get through it. Love and dedication we had in abundance, therefore, we got through the hardest part of the transplant journey. I have no doubt that he would have done the same for me if I had been the one who got sick.

At the time of writing this, we are now more than a year post-transplant, and life is slowly returning to a new normal.

Whatever God has in store for us next, we are ready. I pray that life continues to improve, and we have more time together. Our love and our bond is now weaved so tightly, we have become one unit. He suffers, I suffer; I suffer, he suffers.

Don't get me wrong, we are a normal couple with normal disagreements. We choose not to fight, not to allow differences to tear us apart or bring discord in our lives. We both realized long ago, we are not each other's enemy; we are each other's best friend and each other's lifeline.

Our love has become stronger than anything life throws our way. I thank God every day for the miracle of life my husband was given. I am blessed. I will love Robert until my last dying breath.

I will love him in eternity when he and I will be together in Heaven.

May almighty God watch over you and your families. If you remember anything about this book, remember that love conquers all.

Chapter 3

Coping with My Dad's Health Crisis

By Bradley Treuherz

The Accident

When I reflect on the day of the accident and the moments leading up to it, I'm struck by how abruptly everything changed. There was no warning, no indication that our lives were about to be upended. In an instant, everything was different.

Often, in recounting tales such as these, one might use the phrase, "It was just another ordinary day." But for me, this day was far from ordinary. It was a *good* day. At that time, I was a third-year Computer Engineering student at the University of Florida. Though my workload was typically demanding, Thursdays were mercifully light, and on this particular Thursday, I was ahead of my assignments. With only one lecture in the early afternoon, I relished the walk to and from class.

For those familiar with Gainesville, Florida, the nickname "the swamp" is well understood. The heat and humidity can be oppressive, living up to its reputation. Yet, what many don't realize is how beautiful Gainesville can be in the fall. It was October, and this day epitomized the splendor of an autumn day in Gainesville. I can recall gazing up at an azure sky, unmarred by clouds. The sun's warmth was tempered by a cool breeze, and I found myself in an exceptionally bright mood.

After class, I met up with my roommates, Mark and Sergio, to plan our evening. As college students, we couldn't let a good Thursday night go to waste! My brother Brian had just moved into a house near campus, and he and his roommates were hosting a party that night. It sounded like a great time, so we decided to go.

We made a quick stop at the local CVS to grab some beer and snacks. Inside, we were all joking around and enjoying ourselves. The beautiful weather and anticipation of the party had us in high spirits. We got in line to check out. I was first. I paid for my items, and I can recall still being excited about showing my ID to the cashier, as I had just turned twenty-one earlier that year. As Mark and Sergio stepped up to pay, I absentmindedly pulled out my phone—

3 Missed Calls from Claudia

1 Text

I guess I had not felt my phone vibrate (it was still on silent from class earlier that day). I opened the text.

"Call me . . . accident."

"Accident?" What did she mean by accident? Car accident? I silently stepped out of the store to call her back.

Ring . . . ring . . . ring . . . My heart was pounding in my chest, and my hands were starting to sweat.

Ring . . . ring . . . click . . .

All I heard was SOBBING . . . Guttural SOBBING . . . the worst sound I had ever heard in my life.

"Claudia!?? What happened!??"

Indiscernible wailing . . .

"Claudia! Please tell me what happened!?"

"Accident . . . your father . . . "

"Were you in an accident??? Are you guys okay?"

"Car accident . . . no . . . "

"No, you're not okay? I'm sorry Claudia, I can't understand you. Take your time and breathe. What happened??"

"We were in a car accident . . . your father . . . heart attack."

I could barely make out her words between sobs, but I heard "car accident" and "heart attack" as clear as day.

"You were in a car accident?? Dad had a heart attack??"

I didn't believe what I'd heard. I needed confirmation.

"Yes . . . yes . . . "

"Is he okay? Are you okay?"

"No . . . no . . . "

"No!??? Is he alive??"

"I don't . . . I don't know . . . "

"You don't know if he's alive!??"

Right back to indiscernible wailing and sobbing.

"Claudia??? Stay on the phone with me!"

Click. Silence.

I dialed Claudia.

Ring . . . ring . . . ring . . . no answer.

I dialed again.

Ring . . . ring . . . ring . . . no answer.

This continued for what felt like hours.

Silence.

My mind was swirling with so many questions. I had no answers to any of them. *Is he alive? The car accident, my father's heart attack—which one happened first? Did the heart attack cause the accident or was it the other way around? Does it really matter which happened first? Is my father still with us or have I lost him forever? Why would Claudia just hang up on me and leave me not knowing if he's alive or not??*

At this time, I didn't know the extent of *her* injuries. I would later learn that she had suffered a fractured sternum among other injuries and was not in great shape either. My calls continued to go unanswered, each ring echoing my growing despair.

Mark and Sergio walked outside. They were still smiling and joking around . . . *why wouldn't they be?* I didn't say anything, but I guess the sullen look on my face revealed the storm within me. Mark immediately sensed that something was amiss.

"Is everything okay?" Mark questioned with a look of concern.

"My dad and Claudia got into a car accident; he had a heart attack." I didn't say those words. They flowed from my mouth on their own.

"Look at that idiot taking up two spots." Sergio gestured at a poorly parked car and chuckled. He hadn't heard me.

"Sergio." Mark nudged him and the smile faded from Sergio's face as he picked up on the tension.

"Wait, what?" Mark questioned again.

I don't know if I had spoken too quietly or if it was just too hard to grasp the first time.

"My dad and Claudia got into a car accident, and he had a heart attack," I repeated. This time the words were mine, but they left a void in my chest . . . as if the breath I used to speak to them wouldn't ever return to me.

"Are they okay?" Mark asked the obvious question.

"I don't know." I didn't.

"You don't know?"

"No. That's all I know."

Silence.

Sergio leaned forward to give me a hug, but I shrugged him off. To this day, I still don't know why I rejected the hug. It kind of bothers me, actually. It was a kind gesture, and upon reflection, it was rude of me to push him away. At that moment, I just wanted to be alone with my thoughts.

I started shivering, but I wasn't cold.

"I need to call my brother," I said. He needed to know what was going on.

Ring, ring, ring.

Ring, ring, ring. "Hello?"

"Hi, Brian."

"What's up?" There was a lot of noise in the background. The party had already started.

"Umm . . . " *How do I even start?* "Dad and Claudia got into a car accident."

"What? Are you serious?? Are they okay?"

"I don't know, but Dad had a heart attack." Again, saying those words out loud left me with a strange feeling . . . I was saying the words, but the reality of the situation hadn't quite set in yet.

"What!? Is he okay?"

"I don't know."

"What do you mean you don't know??"

"I don't know . . . I talked to Claudia briefly, but she was sobbing and barely got the words out. The call ended abruptly, and I've been trying to call back but she's not answering."

"Oh my God."

There was a long pause . . . What do you even say?

"Did the heart attack cause the accident or did he crash and then have a heart attack?" Brian asked.

I found it a little funny how we both had almost the same thought. I guess twins do think alike.

"I don't know Brian, I told you everything I know."

"Okay, well f$*k."

I suggested that he come over and stay at my place for a bit. His place was a zoo with the party and neither of us were in any frame of mind to be in that environment.

I got back into Mark's Jeep, and we drove home. I kept trying to call Claudia over and over again but got no answer. For more than twenty minutes I tried calling and for more than twenty minutes I still did not know if my dad had even survived the crash.

He might be dead right now. Did I just lose my dad??

This weird thought popped into my head. When I was a kid, my dad always took great pleasure in teaching me and my brother about science and physics and I immediately thought back to Erwin Schrödinger's thought experiment on the paradox of quantum superposition.

If you are not familiar, the paradox of Schrödinger's Cat is pretty simple. There are a few variations of the experiment, but in the most commonly taught variant a cat is placed into a closed box with a flask of poison, a radioactive source, and a radiation detector (hypothetically of course, at least I hope so—poor cat). When the radioactive source decays, the monitor is triggered, which shatters the flask, releasing the poison and killing the cat.

To an outside observer who cannot see into the box, it is not clear if the radioactive source has already decayed (killing the cat) or has yet to decay (leaving the cat very much alive). Schrödinger argued that the cat is in a state of superposition where it is both dead and alive until the box is opened and the cat can be observed.

My dad is still in the box, I thought. *Both dead and alive.*

I have a Schrödinger dad, I thought and almost cracked a smile. I immediately felt guilty for this, but upon reflection afforded myself the comedic relief. As a matter of fact, I think my dad would have found this analogy funny as well and wouldn't be offended by my use of humor as a coping mechanism. That was the last time I smiled for the rest of the night.

Ring, ring, ring.

Ring, ring, ring.

"Your call has been forwarded to an automated—"
Click.

Ring, ring, ring.

Ring, ring, ring . . .

"Come on, Claudia, please answer!!"

Ring, ring, ring . . .

"Hi . . . Brad."

"Claudia! What's going on, are you guys okay??"

" . . . ."

"Claudia?? I can't understand what's going on. Is he alive??"

"Your . . . fath—"

"Hello??"

Click.

So close . . . *Come on, Claudia! Please!!!! I need to know if he's okay!!*

Ring, ring, ring.

Ring, ring, ring.

"Hello?" An unfamiliar man answered the phone.

Surprised, I asked, "Hi, who is this?"

"Hi, I'm a paramedic," he said calmly. "Your mom handed me the phone here."

Finally, someone I can talk to!

"What's going on?? Is everything okay?"

"Well as you know there's been an accident, and your mom and dad are a little banged up here."

Banged up? Interesting choice of words.

"Is my dad okay?" The million-dollar question!! Open the box!

"Well, he took a pretty hard impact in the crash, and he had an M.I., but we're doing everything we can."

But is he alive?? Let me be more direct.

"Is he alive!??"

"Oh, yeah, he's alive!"

Wow . . . he's alive! For the first time since this whole thing, I heard that he's alive!

"He's right here with me; we're taking good care of him."

"Is he stable?? Is he conscious??"

"Yeah, he's stable right now. I can put him on for you real quick."

Wow . . . I did not expect to be able to talk to him. In fact, I didn't know if I would *ever* talk to him again.

"Hello?" I heard my dad's voice . . . faintly. He sounded so frail.

"Dad! It's Bradley, are you okay?"

What a silly question. Of course he's not okay.

"Bradley," he whispered, "my dear son . . . I've been better."

I didn't know what to say. He sounded so weak. I knew this wouldn't be a long conversation so I said the only words I could think of—the only words that really mattered in a moment like this.

"I love you, Dad."

"I love . . . you . . . too," he replied between labored breaths.

The paramedic took the phone back. "Alright Bradley, I'm gonna let you go so I can take care of your folks." When the paramedic spoke, I was shocked at the juxtaposition of his voice to my father's. He sounded so strong.

"Okay, thank you."

Click.

He's alive!

The First Code

"Your father coded," Claudia said. "He's on a ventilator. You guys should come as soon as you can."

My heart sank when I answered the phone and heard Claudia utter those words. I had enough understanding from having grown up with a physician for a father to know what that meant.

My brother Brian and I were on the next flight out. It had been two weeks since the initial accident. Brian and I had been planning to come out to visit, but I had a big test, and we had planned to leave after. The test could wait now. My father had been fighting to stay alive these past weeks, with life and death trading blows with one another. The fight had taken a turn we hoped it wouldn't, and I was sick to my stomach that I had waited so long to come out.

I should have flown out right away. I would have, had I really understood how dire things were. Brian and I both had rigorous schedules, him on a pre-pharmacy route and myself in the trenches of an engineering degree. We had planned to visit as soon as we could. Well life had other plans, and our course work could be made up. I just hoped it wasn't too late.

The first flight we could find was at 7:00 a.m. the next day. Needless to say, we didn't sleep much that night. Immediately before boarding the flight, I spoke with Claudia for an update on his condition. Things were unclear. He was alive and had a heartbeat but was not yet breathing on his own.

I can remember the uncertainty of the flight. Six and a half hours to get across the country, all the while without cell phone service. Without contact. Not knowing if there was a change in his condition—for better or worse—for six and a half hours. Part of me thought I would land to find that he was already gone, and we were too late.

In my world, he was both alive and dead. Once again left in the paradox where my father's life, unobserved by me, straddled both planes of existence.

After we touched down, I was relieved to discover that his condition had improved slightly and I would be seeing my father, very much alive, shortly.

We entered the hospital and found his room. A priest was there with him. This felt like a bad omen. I gave him privacy before entering, imagining that the priest was administering some form of last rights, or a final confession to absolve my father of his sins prior to his inevitable passing. It seemed my imagination was not too far from the truth.

I entered the room to find a man whom I could hardly recognize. Yet still, laying in bed in front of me was undeniably my father. It had only been two weeks, but he must have lost thirty pounds, if not more. He looked sallow and withdrawn; the skin on his face looked loose, as if draped over his face like a mask rather than a part of it.

His breaths were short and shallow, like he could not catch his breath, even at rest. He couldn't. His hypoxic state manifested in his purple lips and lifeless complexion. He looked like he had seen a ghost, or rather he had *been* a ghost, and wasn't sure how long he would be permitted to remain in his flesh form. He appeared more like a wax sculpture of my father rather than the real deal—an uncanny valley sort of effect where I knew this was my dad, but somehow it wasn't—and it was hard to put my finger on what the missing piece was. It made me feel sick to my stomach.

He was too weak to speak. He tried to, but quickly drew short of breath. The monitors were beeping as his blood oxygen saturation dropped into the mid-seventies.

My eyes met his and he expressed to me, in that moment, more than could ever be expressed through words alone. An exchange of meaningful glances became the medium through which we communicated. This was okay. Despite the vast range of human language, there really weren't enough words. Or at least I couldn't think of any combination of words which could adequately express what we were thinking or feeling. So, we stuck to telepathic communication, so to speak, and sat in silence.

I stayed in LA for about a week, visiting my father every day until he was eventually discharged. None of us felt he was ready to go home, but there wasn't much else to be done for him in the hospital. My dad and Claudia were living in the San Bernardino Mountains in California at that time, at an elevation of about 6,000 feet. The air was thin, and they were far from high quality medical care. That would need to change—the first of countless major life changes to come.

We settled into my grandparents' home in Toluca Lake, California, at sea level and close to both UCLA and Providence Saint Joseph Medical Center, two facilities that would soon become the setting for many of our future life events.

Every day was a battle, an uncertainty. His heart had experienced significant transmural damage. That means the damage to his heart spanned throughout the entire thickness of the heart muscle, from outer to inner layer. This is considered the most severe form of myocardial infarction as it involves end-to-end necrosis of the heart muscle. His heart's ability to function as a pump and move blood through his body had been significantly diminished. It's hard to describe how debilitating an injury of this nature is if you haven't seen it before. This fundamentally impacts every aspect of everything in your life.

Imagine the feeling of having finished a high intensity run and you are completely winded and struggling to catch your breath. Now imagine you ALWAYS feel this way, even while laying perfectly still in bed. Along with the panic and fear of being unable to breathe, imagine trying to put on a shirt, put your socks on, or walk up or down the stairs. It was hard to imagine life going on this way. But it did.

The most immediate fear we all had was the high probability of a sudden cardiac death event. With his heart damaged as it was, the risk of going into an arrhythmia (such as V-tach or V-fib like he did in the hospital), was extremely high. He would need to have an implanted cardioverter defibrillator (ICD) and pacemaker installed. However, for the first few weeks he was too weak for this surgery.

He would have to wear a cardiac LifeVest, or what we came to call a "shock vest." This is just what it sounds like. The LifeVest is a personal defibrillator that one wears (like a vest) that monitors your heart and will deliver a shock if it senses an abnormal heart rhythm. This was a terrifying thought, seconded only by the thought of not having the vest on, which was necessary to shower. I remember how terrifying every shower was, thinking, *this will be the moment it happens.* It wasn't. Thankfully.

The shock vest was simply a bridge to ensure he stayed alive long enough to receive the ICD and pacemaker, which he did shortly after. That was a relief, but that didn't "fix" the problem. It was more like an insurance policy than a solution. He still had a damaged heart, and life was still irreversibly and permanently changed forever.

The first few weeks were almost, in some ways, easier than the weeks to come. The initial shock (no pun intended) of what had just happened kept us energized and going. You have adrenaline. It doesn't really feel real yet. You are just doing what needs to be done to stay alive. When the shock wears off, you are left with the reality of what is and of what will be. The reality wasn't good. Well, I guess it could have been worse.

It was starting to look like my dad would survive this. But for how long and what degree of quality of life he could expect seemed bleak at best. My father went from being a reasonably strong and healthy man to a medical cripple. The cocktail of medications required every day to keep him alive was sickening and made him feel ill. His heart was not going to get better. Rather, he would have to learn to adapt to a deficient heart. Things would not be easy.

At the same time, I was starting to see a new side of my dad and Claudia that I perhaps had not seen before. I was seeing a side of resilience, of determination, of love, and of a willingness to fight. They both loved life, and they loved each other. And they loved their life together. Despite the odds (and there were many people who told us the odds were immeasurably against us), they would fight for a happy and healthy life together. Because there is no other option.

The things they would go through over the next few years could be measured against your worst night-mares. It's hard to wrap my mind around. But despite all this, they did manage to find joy in life. They've both expressed that some of the happiest years of their lives had actually been during this time period.

Eventually my brother and I had to return to school, but we would be back many times over the next ten years. There would be many more grief-stricken phone calls. Many more emergency last-minute flights, and too many fights for survival.

Many More Shocks

I would receive many more phone calls like that one throughout the next ten years, to the point where an unexpected text or call from Claudia would cause my heart to skip a beat. Thankfully, the ICD/pacemaker delivered the lifesaving shock time and time again and brought him back from the edge of life.

There were some close calls though, like losing consciousness while driving. We got lucky that time and he stopped driving after that. There were a few falls and we're thankful to have not had any major injuries. The real fear was that the next time it happened, the shock wouldn't bring him back. There was no guarantee. Devices malfunction, and even when working as expected may not be enough to return his heart to normal sinus rhythm.

During this period, a large focus of my life became dedicated to my father's health—both physical, emotional, and spiritual. There were many "drop everything and get on a flight" moments. Many late-night phone calls. The fragility of life became a daily awareness. Most healthy young men in their early twenties are fortunate enough not to have to think about such things—most have experienced some loss, but somehow this felt different. The very nature of the accident, and the sudden, unexpected onset of the additional cardiac events, brought with it a feeling of "this could happen at any moment."

I thought often about my father's life and how tenuous its continuation was. I thought about my own life, made acutely aware of how much of a gift it is to be healthy.

To recount every near-death incident would be an arduous task . . . to be honest, they all seem to blend together.

What I do remember distinctly is how spontaneously it happened every time. Out of the blue. No warning or care for the plans we had made or the intentions we had set forward. It was hard to plan for things out of fear that something might happen (and it often did). For many years, my dad and Claudia were afraid to make plans. There were a few rare occasions where they had attempted to take a vacation, only to have their plans foiled time and time again by unexpected medical disasters.

Other Life-Threatening Incidents

The cardiac incidents were somehow not the only life-threatening events to occur. There was one time—I happened to be visiting when it happened—where I found my father doubled over on the floor in the living room . . . writhing in pain. This wasn't heart-related but rather a gallstone had positioned itself into his pancreatic duct, facilitating a gallstone pancreatitis. Gallstone pancreatitis is a life-threatening emergency requiring immediate, life-saving surgery.

My father had cancer. I remember sitting with him in the oncology suite while he prepared for his radiation treatments. As if this wasn't enough by itself, the treatment was made much more complicated by his defibrillator, which needed to be turned off while the treatment was in progress. This was a scary thought, as we knew his heart could betray him at any moment. We were fortunate that he had no cardiac issues during his many radiation treatment sessions.

The Bear

He also had two hip fractures. The first one occurred in an almost unbelievable fashion. My dad was walking our dogs, when they came across a black bear. The bear got spooked by Max, our German shepherd, and, in an attempt to run away from Max, was charging on a direct path towards my dad.. Knowing the temperament of black bears, especially in this area, I think it's very unlikely the bear was trying to cause harm to my dad . . . though when cubs are involved all bets are off. Either way, it's hard not to be afraid when a large bear is charging right towards you!

My dad ran away and fell, fracturing his left hip in the process. Thankfully the bear was in fact uninterested in him (he was trying to get away from Max). My dad lay on the ground for about twenty minutes, unable to move until Claudia realized he hadn't returned from walking the dogs and found him.

The Spinal Tumor

The second hip fracture, though it doesn't make quite as riveting a story as running from a bear, was much scarier.

At this point, I had almost gotten used to the "medical emergency" phone call from Claudia. I wouldn't say it had become routine, but we had experience now.

"Your father fell, he broke his hip, we're on the way to Providence St. Joseph's Medical Center in Burbank." Claudia relayed the information very matter-of-factly.

"Is he okay, can I talk to him?"

"Hi Brad, I'm okay." He went on to describe what had happened and assured me he was fine.

But something struck me about the way that he spoke. I could pick up on something in his voice that felt unsettling. I couldn't quite put my finger on it. There was no fear or panic, as you might expect from someone experiencing a traumatic fracture. In fact, I think it was the absence of such emotions that made me feel uneasy. Instead, what I found in its place was a much more unsettling brand of . . . irritation? He seemed . . . inconvenienced. Just another thing to deal with.

There was the three-plus hour drive to and from the hospital, *who can we get to watch the dogs? How long will I be on a "no food or water" order from the doctors while I'm waiting to get into the schedule (that was always a major pain in the ass).* There were practical considerations, and a spontaneous hip fracture wasn't part of the plan.

He had just "mis-stepped" in the kitchen and fell while walking to the trash can. His brain told his foot to move, but it lagged. Just for a split second, but it was enough for his foot to drag and catch on the ground. He lost his balance and fell, landing with his full weight directly on his right hip.

It fractured; without a question of a doubt, it was fractured. He accepted this and immediately became resigned to the situation. After all, he had been here before.

But why had he fallen? Maybe that's what I had picked up on earlier in our conversation. There was a missing piece—the elephant in the room. The hip could be taken care of. Compared to the heart procedures he had been through, that was simple carpentry.

The reason for his fall occupied a lot of space in our minds. Despite his limited cardiac output, my dad was always steady on his feet. He wasn't the feeble old man one expects to be a fall risk. This was out of character.

Ever since his last ablation procedure, he had been experiencing pain in his right shoulder. This was accompanied by numbness and decreased mobility in his right arm. It seemed reasonable to expect that this was a complication from the surgery. During the ablation procedure, his body had been held in strange positions for long periods of time. We thought maybe a nerve had been compressed or that this was some facet of the recovery process that would get better with time.

It did not get better. It got worse.

Itstartedtoimpacthisabilitytoplaythepiano—something

extremely frustrating as he loves to play (and we all love to listen). He also started experiencing some neuropathy in his legs and began to have difficulties with balance. He had scheduled an MRI to look for an explanation.

The hip fracture happened a week before his MRI. Looks like he would be getting that MRI a little early.

I was shopping at the local Fred Meyers for groceries when I got the call. I answered; Claudia was crying.

"I have the results of the MRI," she informed me. "I just sent them to you."

Uh oh. Hearing Claudia crying because of imaging results was *not* a good sign. As she uttered those words, my phone vibrated in my hand. I opened the screenshots she had sent me on MyChart and started to read the text.

I remember reading "Intradural Extramedullary Mass" and "severely compressing the spinal cord." I felt a surge of adrenaline as I read through the report. I started pacing through the store aisles.

My dad had just finished radiation treatment for prostate cancer only a few months earlier . . . *and now there's a mass in his spine!?*

I had so many questions, but Claudia didn't have the answers. We just had the report. I'm not a doctor, and neither is she. I've learned to be very careful when trying to interpret medical test results. It's very easy to jump to conclusions and misinterpret things you think you understand but don't fully grasp (since you don't have the deep foundation of a medical education required).

I took this report with a grain of salt and tried not to make any assumptions, but it was pretty clear to me that he had a tumor in his spine that was putting pressure on his spinal cord. That would explain the pain and the fall. I still had so many questions.

The *C word* was obviously the first thing that came to mind. *Is it a metastasis from his prostate cancer? Obviously, any tumor is not a good thing, but how bad is this???*

"Please don't tell your father yet," Claudia said, wanting to protect him. "He's still lying in the hospital bed with a broken hip."

They hadn't taken him for surgery yet to repair his hip—the most "urgent" medical issue at the moment. "The last thing he needs is to be worrying about this," she said. "He needs to be able to focus on recovering from this surgery first."

I thought about this. As a general rule, I always favor full transparency in communication. It's hard for me to hide things like this from him, or from anybody. I didn't want to.

But I thought about him waking up in recovery after the hip surgery in a state of semi-consciousness and confusion. If he knew about the spinal tumor before the surgery, would he remember it then? Of course, not right away. But then again, he would certainly remember eventually.

What about during the time in between? I imagined him in a dream-like state, starting to remember the diagnosis. Half aware, half unaware, perhaps recalling and then forgetting his diagnosis multiple times before becoming fully alert. Each occurrence would be like hearing the news for the first time, over and over. I imagined him having demented thoughts and hallucinations from the strong narcotics he would surely be on post-op, not knowing what was real and what wasn't.

Fine. He doesn't need to know right now.

"Okay, I won't tell him," I said over a lot of background noise. She was crying. "Where are you now?"

"I had to leave. I opened the report on my phone in the room with him and had to walk out. I couldn't handle it and broke down. I didn't want him to see me. He would know something happened."

Claudia sounded like she was having a panic attack. Maybe I was, too.

"Are you driving right now?" I asked, worried about her behind the wheel under such intense emotional distress.

"Yes! I didn't have a choice. I couldn't stay there. I'm going home."

Home was more than two hours away. I urged her to drive safely and pull over for a moment, but she insisted she would be okay and continued on her way home.

There was no way I could change Claudia's mind about anything, and this was no exception.

"Dad's calling me. I need to go." I hung up and answered the incoming call from my father.

"Dad, how are you feeling? Is everything okay?" I tried to keep my voice under control.

"I've been better, but I'm worried about Claudia."

Classic. He was in some horrendous state of disease, and his first thought was about the well-being of his wife.

"I think she's having a hard time handling this," Dad said. "She just stormed off crying out of nowhere and went home."

Oh, man. He knows something's up. How could he not? I don't like being put in this position where I have to keep things from him. But the image of him battling post-op delirium with the knowledge that "the worst is yet to come" grounded me and assured me that this was the right thing.

"Yeah, I know," I said. "I just got off the phone with her."

There was no reason to lie . . . I just wouldn't tell him everything.

"Oh yeah?" he asked. "How did she sound to you?"

"Not very good," I said.

"I wonder what happened? She just lost it all of a sudden.

One moment we were here together, and out of nowhere, she's crying and running out."

He didn't really suspect that she knew something. He

had no reason to. He was just concerned for her well-being.

"I mean," I said, "this must be hard for her.

To see the man she loves in pain. How much of that can you expect someone to take before they break?"

"Yeah, I guess so," he said.

"In some ways," he continued, "I think these hospitalizations have been harder on her than they have been on me. All I have to do is lay here. She has to watch the person she loves suffer again and again."

"It's been hard on both of you," I said. "I don't think there's anything to be gained by arguing whose suffering is worse."

"Yeah, I suppose so," Dad added. "We'll get through this."

"Yeah, you will," I said. "Look at what you've been through before; this is nothing."

It wasn't nothing. It wasn't going to be nothing. That was the first and only lie I told during our conversation. What was to come was probably the hardest physical recovery process out of all of his experiences so far. But like all the others, we would get through it because we had to.

What was the alternative? To roll over and die? That was not an option. When you think there is nowhere else to go, you start operating on a different wavelength. I guess you could call it "survival mode." Things you wouldn't expect yourself to be able to do or get through, you do, because you're there, and because time goes on.

Eventually, months pass, and you're standing on the other side thinking, *Wow, glad that's over with.* But to get to the other side, you first have to go through it. And we were still at the very start of this one.

I suddenly realized I was standing in the soup aisle, completely spaced out. I didn't even remember what I had come in to get. I quickly checked out with the items I had already acquired and returned home.

The Discovery

He found out about the tumor before we wanted him to know. I guess sometimes we forget he's a doctor, and he picks up on things. The surgery for the hip went fine—routine. As he recovered and regained consciousness, he started to notice things that didn't add up. Or perhaps he had started to notice things that *did* add up. And he was beginning to calculate the sum.

There were additional tests and labs ordered that he picked up on—blood tests for neoplastic markers, additional imaging of the c-spine, etc. *Why had a neuro-surgeon come to see him three times that day? Why was nobody talking about the results of his MRI?*

The Phone Call

Ring, ring, ring.

(I had already spoken to my dad a few times since he

came out of surgery, and he was fully alert.)

"Hi Dad, how are you feeling?"

"I've been better. Look, I gotta tell you something, but please don't tell Claudia."

Uh oh. Of course, in this moment, his first thought was to protect Claudia and keep her from worrying.

"Yeah, sure. What's going on?"

"I think they found something on the MRI. A mass in my spine."

Yup. He had figured it out.

"Oh no. What did they say?"

"Nobody has said anything to me yet, but I've had three neurosurgeons come in to evaluate my case, and something doesn't seem right. It seems like the only logical conclusion."

Alright. He had figured it out.

We had hoped to give him at least a full day to recover before breaking the news. But at this point, there was no reason to continue the farce. I thought of how to phrase it— how to make it go down easier. It felt like we were beyond the point of trying to sugarcoat things. The faster we could merge our collective realities, the sooner we could move on to getting through this as a unit. In this case, direct and clear language would be the most effective.

"Yes, you do," I said plainly. "I saw the report. Claudia sent it to me."

"You already knew?? Wha—"

"Claudia and I both saw it last night while you were awaiting the surgery. That's why she ran out of the room. We discussed it and felt that the additional stress of the news immediately pre- and post-op was not in your best interest."

It seemed as though his gut instinct was to protest. But intellectually, he understood and agreed that this was probably the right call. We went on to discuss the details of the report.

Denial and Survival Mode

There's a lot of emotion that goes through your head—both as the bearer of this information and especially as the person who has the tumor. But I've learned in times of extreme crisis like this, the human body and mind protect themselves.

Some might call it the denial stage of grief, but I think that's an oversimplification and frankly a pessimistic way of looking at it. I think it's something beautiful, actually—or if not beautiful, at least fascinating. The ability to, for a time, repress all those emotions and simply resign yourself to "getting through it."

What will come, will come. What will be, will be. And we will continue to be, until we are not.

Again, there was no choice but to get through it. And we were prepared for battle yet again.

Though, as we would all learn later, that repression of emotions to "just get through it" is very much a non-sustainable and temporary state of being. Some people stay in that state for too long and end up paying the price. PTSD, anxiety, therapy—eventually, facing and working through those emotions *must* come. But not yet.

First, we would bear down and get through it. I think recognizing the need to transition out of this state has been one of the most helpful observations I've made in understanding why this ordeal has been so challenging for us all.

A Non-Malignant But Dangerous Tumor

The tumor was benign—thank God. I suppose we wouldn't know for sure until it was biopsied; however, based on the characteristics of the tumor the doctors seemed very confident in reassuring us of that fact.

However, malignancy aside, it was still a tumor. And it was still in his spine. And it was still compressing his spinal cord. Though I must say, this news made us lighter.

Cancer or not, the tumor was life-threatening and needed to be taken care of as soon as possible. Once he had stabilized from the hip surgery (about a week later), he would go in for surgery to remove the tumor.

The Spinal Surgery and Recovery

The tumor was excised, but the surgery was not without complications. He went into the surgery with pain and weakness in his right arm and came out with the arm completely numb and fully paralyzed.

Would feeling and movement come back? There were no definitive answers. The response seemed to depend on who we asked:

"Most likely."

"We'll have to see."

"I hope so."

These were the closest things to affirmations we could get—and they weren't very reassuring. At this point, the prognosis was essentially the same as someone who had come into the emergency room from a traumatic accident with a spinal cord injury.

Months of intense inpatient physical rehabilitation would follow—rehabilitation made all the more difficult by a dying heart that was struggling to supply the body with the oxygen-rich blood it needed to heal.

Learning to Walk Again

I spent a lot of time with my dad in the rehab unit and really saw what it looks like for a man to fight to get his life back. He had to learn how to walk again.

You know, I've heard people say the phrase "learn

how to walk again" in various contexts following injuries or major surgeries. But it's hard to describe what that actually means unless you're there.

How does one "forget" how to walk? You *know* how to walk, right? It's just a matter of getting your strength back, right?

Wrong.

It can be much more than that.

Breaking and Rebuilding Connections

During spinal cord injuries, the connection between your brain and your muscles becomes fundamentally different from what it was before.

What does it mean to "know" how to walk? Well, it means that your brain understands the pathways and signals it needs to send to move your muscles in the correct sequence. A lot of those signals happen without requiring much conscious thought—like making micro-adjustments to preserve balance.

When those pathways are broken due to a spinal cord injury, the pathways your brain is used to using don't work like they used to. Your brain must relearn how to send those signals, and that requires conscious effort—both mentally and physically.

Gabriel, The Guardian Angel

My dad had the privilege of working with an amazing therapist while in rehab named Gabriel (who he often referred to as his guardian angel). There was one session in particular where my dad was really struggling.

Gabriel stopped the walk, sat us down, and pulled out a book on the mechanics of walking. Together, we studied, in detail, the phases of the normal gait cycle. My dad literally had to learn—not just physically, but academically, from a textbook—how to walk again.

And he did walk again.

I watched him move from a wheelchair to a walker, to a cane, to finally having the confidence and stability to walk unassisted.

The Arm That Never Fully Came Back

However, as the months went on, his right arm remained paralyzed, and our hope for a full recovery slowly dwindled.

He had gained back grip strength and could move his fingers. His tricep control had returned as well, but he had no ability whatsoever to raise or rotate his arm. My dad is right-handed, and he lost most of the function of his right arm. I can't even imagine how frustrating that would make daily life. But he learned to adapt.

He started using his left arm to position his weak arm wherever he needed it and relied on his grip strength or "crawled" his arm around using his fingers.

He even began to play the piano again by propping his arm up on the edge of the keys. It wasn't the same, but he could play. He would play.

And that's what mattered.

The Transplant Journey

I was living in Seattle when I got the call. I had been on "standby" mode in anticipation of the call, but I wasn't really expecting it to come so soon. The call came on Valentine's Day (what a strange and beautiful coincidence) just three weeks after his acceptance to the program. Three weeks is an extremely short amount of time to wait in the transplant world, so I didn't exactly have everything together.

I had planned to relocate via the twenty-hour drive down the coast. That would make things easier. I would have my truck down there with me and didn't really have to think too hard about packing. That made preparing for the move MUCH easier!

I "packed" in the most efficient way I could think at the time, which pretty much meant I just threw everything I thought I might need for the next six months into the back of my truck: clothes, my guitar, snowboard, surfboard, and all my work stuff. I felt kind of silly bringing all this stuff as I knew this wasn't going to be a vacation.

I didn't know if I would even have time to use them and that certainly wasn't going to be a priority. Still, snowboarding and surfing bring me a lot of joy, and this whole experience has taught me to never miss an opportunity to fill your life with things that bring you happiness. I had plenty of space in the bed of my Ranger, and it was hard to anticipate how long I would need to be there . . . better to have it and not use it than wish I had taken them with me. I managed to get everything together that evening and was on the road at first light the next morning.

I wanted to be there when my dad woke up from surgery. I wanted to hold his hand and assure him that he was safe, and everything was okay. That wasn't logistically possible, and I had to accept that early on or the drive would have seemed endless. Besides, he didn't really need me then . . . he had the full support of the amazing medical staff at the UCLA transplant center along with the support of his wife Claudia. When he would really need me was during the weeks and months to come after. I would be there for him then and that's what really mattered. I realized I self-ishly wanted to be there more for myself than for him. I wanted to be part of the process and felt left out by not being there. As a matter of fact, it really would have made no difference to him at all as he wasn't even conscious for the first couple days.

There were some complications during the surgery, and he was kept in a medically induced coma for the first day and a half, but more on that later. I battled internally with the sense of urgency that came with my rapid departure juxtaposed against the laborious twenty-hour drive I had before me. I found myself wishing time away . . . wishing to be there already. Ironically, this goes against one of the core tenets of my father's own value system—to live NOW and allow yourself to be totally and fully consumed by the experience of the present moment. I thought about this and found the best way to honor my father at a time like this was to try to embrace the moment as best as I could. With this thought, I found myself focusing on the now and realized that I was actually enjoying the drive.

I listened to JRR Tolken's *The Fellowship of the Ring* audiobook. I had seen the movies before but never read the book and this seemed like a good opportunity to take my mind off things. As Frodo started embarking on his perilous journey, I found parallels between his journey and my own. The west coast of the United States is absolutely gorgeous and traversing its countryside makes one feel as though they are on an epic voyage as well.

I departed Seattle during a snowstorm (which really only happens a few times a year at sea level). This added a sense of thrill (though I think there may have already been enough of that). The Pacific Northwest is beautiful, and I watched the weather and topography change as I made my way down Washington, across the Columbia River, and into Oregon. I found myself marveling at the beauty of the redwood forests as I reached Northern California and was completely blown away by the stunning beauty of Mt. Shasta.

While driving from Seattle to Los Angeles, Bradley took this photograph of Mt. Shasta in Northern California, which is a spiritual and sacred site for many people. This area has special meaning because I lived there for a year while doing my fourth year of medical school through UC-Davis at Mt. Shasta General Hospital.

I watched crop dusters perform (what seemed to me to be) daring low-altitude maneuvers, and helicopters performing repairs on massive high voltage power lines as I passed through the farmlands of northern California. It's hard not to be consumed by fear and anxiety while embarking on a journey of this purpose, but I truly found myself living in the now and thoroughly enjoying the moment; something I think my dad would be very proud of. I drove for fourteen hours straight the first day before stopping at a motel somewhere between Sacramento and Stockton. I picked up again first thing the following morning and arrived at the UCLA medical center six hours later.

Arrival at the Hospital

I arrived to find my father having only just recently been awakened and taken off the ventilator. It had been more than a full day since the surgery was completed and he hadn't been able to start breathing on his own until now. One of the nurses informed us that his new heart was "very weak," and it was taking him a little longer than expected to bounce back. I was desperately trying to get a better understanding of what that meant.

Why was his new heart weak? Isn't this supposed to be the new strong heart that we've all been hoping for? Is this a normal part of the transplant process, or has something gone wrong?

It was hard to pinpoint exactly what it was, but something felt off. The nurses and doctors spoke to us with very guarded language that seemed to have an undertone of tempering our expectations of his recovery. They spoke very matter-of-factly about the present state of things but made little or no comments about what to expect in the future. Even then, it took multiple rounds of asking several doctors until I finally found one willing to paint a clear picture of what was actually going on.

"The new heart came all the way from Texas," the attending informed us, "and had a cold ischemic time of about six hours."

Cold ischemic time is the measure of how long an organ is chilled without a blood supply between removal from the donor and transplantation in the recipient. He went on, "Typically four hours would be considered the upper limit, but this heart was transported using a SherpaPack, which allows for organs to remain viable with longer ischemic times."

He seemed to read my mind and answered my question before I asked it when he said: "Don't worry, this is *still* a good heart. We wouldn't have accepted it if we weren't fully confident that we would have a good outcome with this heart. But six hours is pretty much the upper limit for us here even with the SherpaPack transport system."

The doctor's words took the air out of the room.

"We had a hard time getting the new heart to start," he said. "Usually, we like to see the heart start beating again on its own once it is warmed and the blood supply is returned. That didn't happen here, at least not with the strength and coordination required to support life."

We were all too stunned to speak, so we just listened as the doctor continued:

"The transplant surgeon had to keep his chest open and massage the heart for over an hour, manually pumping the heart to ensure proper perfusion of the stunned cardiac tissue. Don't be alarmed, while this wasn't something we expected, it's not terribly uncommon and the heart is working fine now. The new heart is still a little stunned and will take some time to recover."

Wow. That put everything into focus and the last few days made a little more sense. I looked over at my father. He looked like he was barely alive, or rather, was only alive at the present moment thanks to the delicate balance of complex medical management he was receiving.

He was on max doses of pretty much every vasopressor and inotrope you could think of. The typical IV pole we had come to expect from his hospitalizations had been replaced with a complex network of various machines and devices. He had multiple IVs on both hands and wrists, a central line/ tube the size of a garden hose going into his neck (a Swan-Ganz catheter). He had metal leads going into his heart, as he required a temporary external pacemaker to control the rhythm of his new heart. He had three large tubes going into three separate holes in his chest and abdomen, connected to a pump to drain blood from his thoracic cavity. There was a fourth tube about the same size connected to a wound vac placed on his chest, and of course another tube for his foley came from under his gown to drain urine from his bladder.

This wasn't over yet. We very much got the feeling that the proverbial "corner" had not yet been turned, and the nurses and doctors made very few promises that one was guaranteed.

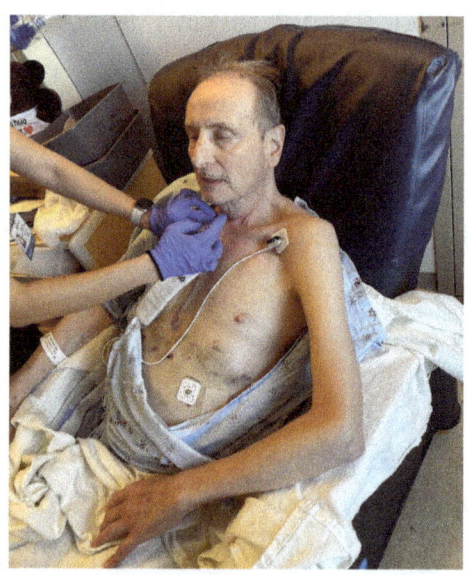

This photo was taken eight days after my heart transplant. A short time later, I would be re-admitted for a rejection scare.

Eventually, and by the grace of God, he did turn that corner. It wasn't like a light switch, but rather a slow and gradual improvement, which occurred a little bit every day. Maybe "occurred" isn't the right word, as it implies that his recovery somehow happened on its own. It didn't. It might be better to say that his slow and gradual improvement had been *achieved* a little bit every day. The Cambridge Dictionary defines "achieve" as "to successfully bring about or reach a desired goal, result, or level of success through *effort, skill,* or *courage.*"

Yeah, that's much more appropriate. His health had been *achieved* thanks to the skill of the transplant team and thanks to his courage and the heroic efforts he made to get better every day. I can assure you from having been here that heroic efforts were being made at every hour and minute of the day. I was with him the first time he stood up after the surgery, and boy, what a heroic effort that was. I was also there pretty much every time after that too and it didn't seem to get any easier, especially as he graduated from standing to walking.

Every time he had to cough (keep in mind that his sternum had been cracked open and was being held together with wires), it required tremendous effort, strength of will, and the courage to endure certain pain. But he had to cough. As a doctor, he knew that if he couldn't clear his lungs, he would likely develop pneumonia and not make it out of there. So, he coughed, and he walked, and he got better.

It wouldn't be fair to attribute his recovery to pure effort and strength of will alone. He had some of the most intelligent, attentive, and highly trained medical experts one could ever hope for. I had always assumed that the surgery itself was the most complicated part of a heart transplant. But after witnessing the process, I realized that post-transplant medical management is equally, if not more, technically challenging and involved.

The sheer amount of medication he was on post-transplant was astonishing. And by medication, we're not talking about antibiotics taken orally twice daily. These were incredibly complex medications with intricate interactions that required constant dose adjustments. Lab work and other tests were performed hourly, sometimes even by the minute. They went so far as to place a temperature probe in his pulmonary artery to monitor his cardiac output.

With each lab, test result, and measurement, the doctors fine-tuned the medications based on precisely what his body needed at that exact moment. He didn't just have a doctor—he had teams of multiple doctors who met several times daily to discuss his case and adjust his plan of care.

The doctors would convene right outside his room during rounds, and I would often try to listen to their discussions. Most of it went over my head, but I could tell things weren't great during the first few days. As time went on, it seemed like things were improving. I heard them making decisions to lower or discontinue certain medications, which seemed like a positive sign.

There was one particular day when I heard a doctor say something to the effect of, "We are extremely pleased with how he's doing. Everything is going as well as we could possibly hope for."

Wow. What a relief. Things continued to progress in that direction, and less than two weeks after surgery, we received discharge orders. We were getting ready to take him home!

Getting Home

I spend a lot of time praising the efforts and courage of my father and attributing his successful recovery to the skill and expertise of the medical staff. In doing so, I've omitted perhaps the single most significant factor contributing to his success through this whole ordeal—**Claudia.**

Without Claudia, there wouldn't be a story to tell. Or rather, there would be a very short story with a much less happy ending. I could talk about how she was the spiritual and emotional beacon that guided my father through this nightmare, but I'm sure you'll hear plenty of that from his own recounting of these events.

Beyond that, she was also the logistical reason for his successful outcome. When the doctors in Florida told us there was nothing they could do, Claudia was the one who reached out to air ambulance companies to arrange transport. She didn't sit around and wait—she called multiple times daily and pushed for it to happen.

When it became clear that a coordinated transport was unlikely, Claudia changed the game plan. She pulled the plug and booked a commercial flight that got him to UCLA, where they could save his life. She found and booked an Airbnb minutes from the UCLA Medical Center so we could all stay close to the transplant team during the months that followed.

The list goes on and on. Every step of the way, Claudia spoke up and advocated for his health so loudly and unyieldingly that sometimes it even felt embarrassing. But is it embarrassing to have a father who's still alive? Her tenacity in the pursuit of his well-being and the fervent love she has for my father *is* the reason he's alive today. We all see it, we all recognize it, and I am eternally grateful to her for that.

Recovery

Getting back home—or rather, to our new temporary home on Curson Avenue near UCLA—was scary. It felt too soon. Not even two weeks after the heart transplant, and they had already sent him home?! Our nurse Ken informed us that the average hospital stay post heart transplant at UCLA is seven to ten days. That seemed way too short to me, but I guess that's how they do things.

The transplant coordinator told us that everybody

feels this way, and nobody thinks they're ready to go home. Yeah, no kidding. We were kept busy during those first few weeks, which, while physically demanding, helped distract us from the intensity of what had just occurred. The transplant team kept using the term "new normal," and we quickly started to understand why.

The stress of managing the medication regimen alone was enough to cause sleepless nights. My father had grown accustomed to taking a daily cocktail of heart meds, but post-transplant medication management was a new beast altogether.

There were the immunosuppressive medications: Mycophenolate, Tacrolimus, and Prednisone. These were the "core" transplant drugs that essentially shut down his immune system to prevent his body from launching an immune response against the new heart. This is often referred to as rejection—the dreaded "R" word.

These drugs are given in extremely high doses for the first few months, putting him at an incredibly high risk of infection. To mitigate that risk, more medications were required—antivirals, antibiotics, and antifungals. He was also taking medications to control heart rate, blood pressure, and even more drugs to combat the side effects caused by all those other medications.

These medications had to be taken at specific times, sometimes four different times throughout the day.

Some were prescribed with a taper schedule, where the dose changed every few days. There was *so* much to keep up with, and a medication management mistake could be fatal. We had our hands full.

Rejection Scare

We had been home, adjusting to this "new normal," for about two weeks when we got a call from Jonathan, the transplant coordinator. One of the biopsies had shown something they didn't like—*donor-specific antibodies.*

In layman's terms, the body was starting to mount an immune response against the new heart. *Rejection.* Or so I thought in my naive understanding of the term.

Before this process, I had always thought of rejection in transplant patients as binary. Either your body accepts the organ if it's a good match, or it rejects it if it's not. The reality, however, is much more nuanced.

There's no such thing as a truly *perfect* match. Many factors determine if a heart is a good match, but left to its own devices, the recipient's body will always recognize a donor organ as foreign and try to eradicate it. Hence, the immunosuppressive medications.

Rejection is not an all-or-nothing phenomenon. Sure, there are drastic forms of rejection, such as acute or hyperacute rejection, which can happen rapidly. But there are also chronic forms of rejection that occur very slowly over many years. Identifying signs of rejection doesn't necessarily mean the transplant has failed. There are ways to treat rejection and further suppress the immune system to combat the response that was starting to form.

If treated quickly, the prognosis is good. I was beginning to understand that this "new normal" wasn't just about changing routines. It was about accepting certain realities that come with living with a transplanted organ.

Continued Recovery

Thankfully, he responded well to the treatment and only spent a few nights in the hospital. After this round of treatment, we continued to live our "new normal." Little by little, his strength returned. The weekly heart biopsies turned into bi-weekly biopsies, then monthly, and now they aren't even on the schedule!

We started to shift our focus from merely surviving to thriving and enjoying life again. During the first few months, I didn't feel comfortable leaving unless it was absolutely necessary. I was afraid of getting exposed to an illness and not being available if he needed me.

But as the doses of the immune-suppressing medications were tapered and his stamina returned, I started surfing again.

The Wave

I was out on dawn patrol at Sunset Point, hoping to catch some waves before work. I had been having a rough week. The weight of everything felt particularly heavy, and I was growing weary from the quarantine and isolation. I hadn't really wanted to wake up so early, but I forced myself to do so. It was becoming depressing for my days to consist solely of waking up, working, eating, and going to bed.

The waves weren't very big—a small south swell, roughly stomach to chest high—but the tide was low, and there was a light offshore breeze, making for very clean, "glassy" conditions. The paddle out was easy, and I arrived at the point with my hair still dry.

Sunset Point is a mellow wave, often referred to as a "beginner" spot or "longboard" wave. Having mostly surfed relentless beach breaks on the coast of Washington and during storms in Florida, this was a welcome reprieve. I was riding a five-foot, eleven-inch quad-fin fish that day, which would be very at home in the mushy surf.

The sun was just starting to come out, and there were only a few other surfers in the lineup. After waiting for a few minutes, I saw a shadow on the horizon, signaling that a set was coming. The first wave of the set arrived, and my board rose up and down as it passed under me.

126

One of the other surfers took off and rode it swiftly down the line. I had surfed here a couple times and recognized a few of the guys in the lineup as surfers local to the area. They were generally very friendly, unlike the "locals" at some of the other spots around here. Still, I knew better than to try to take the first wave of the set and patiently waited for my turn.

Though, as the second wave of the set came, I found myself closest to the peak and one of the locals called me into the wave. I was in the perfect spot, and it only took a few paddle strokes before I felt the wave pick me up and push me forward. I popped up to my feet and turned to the right, setting my rail and angling my board down the line. The waves at sunset are very mellow and of low consequence, but if you time it right they peel down the line, staying open for a long time and offering a fairly long ride. I pumped down the line, turning from the bottom of the wave up the face to meet the lip, then back down again, using gravity and the energy from the wave to propel me forward.

I'm used to surfing closeout beach breaks, so as I looked down the line, I saw a vision I didn't often get to see—a clean wave face staying open and begging to be ridden. I'm a very average surfer (at best), so I didn't do any radical maneuvers. The wave was slow and mellow and offered no opportunities to get barreled or anything like that. But the wave held its shape and allowed me to link together several top-to-bottom turns.

I found myself generating too much speed and getting away from the pocket of the wave (which has the most power). I cut back toward the white water and turned again to angle my board back down the line. After a few more pumps, I saw a section ahead of me start to break that I wouldn't have been able to make it past, so I turned up the shoulder to exit the wave.

As I started my paddle back toward the point, a pod of dolphins surfaced just a few feet from me. They seemed to be playing in the swell, just like I was. I found myself grinning from ear to ear.

Yes! This was it. This was the answer to the question that had been irking me for so long. Not the dolphins, or the waves, or surfing for that matter. But moments like this.

Moments like this bring joy to your life. That's what makes it all worth it.

Surfing brought Bradley joy and helped him cope with the challenges of my health crises. Riding "the wave" on this particular day was especially powerful because he said it exemplified my encouragement to live life to the fullest.

I thought back to my dad and the way he had been living his life through countless trials of courage and will. He wasn't a surfer (I'm not sure if he's ever even been on a surfboard), but that didn't matter. He constantly found and pursued, with passion, moments like that wave—moments that brought him joy.

Even when he was in pain, he found things to focus on that made him smile and laugh. Upon reflecting on this, I remembered a quote from Viktor Frankl in his book *Man's Search for Meaning,* where he chronicles his experiences in a concentration camp during World War II. He said that your circumstances and the direction of your life may be out of your control, but no one can take away your ability to choose how you perceive your experiences. What you CAN control is yourself and your attitude.

Yes, that was how he did it. By choosing to have a positive attitude and focusing on the moments that bring joy, one can endure anything—and be fulfilled and happy while doing so.

In a way, that wave changed my life—or at least the revelations it brought to light for me. It felt like I had found my "meaning of life." Not surfing, but actively pursuing the things *like* surfing that make me happy.

For weeks after that morning, I woke up before sunrise and went surfing every morning before work, splitting my time between the Venice Breakwater and Sunset Point. I even managed to find a weekend—one of the last before the season ended—to make it up to Bear Mountain with my snowboard right after a big snowfall.

Things didn't always go smoothly over the next few months, though. There was another bad test result that resulted in a brief hospitalization and additional treatment to battle "rejection."

But that almost didn't matter.

For as long as we were all alive, we had chosen to be happy and to focus on the things that kept us happy.

Claudia's Hospitalization

There was a period of time when Claudia grew ill and spent a few weeks in the hospital with a debilitating recurrence of diverticulitis. I won't lie—even with this newfound philosophy on life, this still hit us both pretty hard.

It was especially tough on my dad, as he couldn't even visit her due to the exposure risk. Though I had learned the practice of embracing life and pursuing joyful moments in times of crisis from him, in this moment, it felt like *he* needed a reminder.

One day, we had gone together to the UCLA Medical Center in Santa Monica to bring Claudia a few things. Of course, he couldn't come in (hospitals are a breeding ground for infectious disease), but he waited in the car while I quickly ran inside.

I could tell this saddened him, so I surprised him on the way home by stopping briefly at the Museum of Flying near the Santa Monica airport, just a few blocks from the hospital. The museum was mostly empty, and with a mask and gloves, the risk of exposure could be mitigated.

Besides, the emotional necessity of such a thing seemed to outweigh the risks at this moment.

You see, my dad has always had a passion for aviation. He flew gliders as a teenager and made it a considerable way through flight school as a young adult. Life, and most significantly the pursuit of a medical education, got in the way of completing his flight training; but still it left a lasting impression and passion that stuck with him for life.

When my brother and I were children, our father had on several occasions taken us on discovery flights in a small single-engine aircraft. These moments were extremely memorable for us all and were a cherished part of my childhood. Due to the fragility of his condition, it had been decades since he had had the opportunity to fly and I knew he longed for it (he spent hours every day on the Microsoft Flight Simulator in Virtual Reality on a computer I had built for him).

As we were leaving the museum, we happened to pass a flight school, Proteus Air Services. We pulled into the parking lot and walked inside to enquire about Discovery Flights. We left with a discovery flight booked for the following day in a Cirrus SR22T (that is like the Ferrari of single-engine propeller planes). I did have some reservations about whether my father was strong enough for such an activity. We talked about it at length and reached a conclusion that was hard to argue with. He had been pretty stable for a few months and his new heart was strong. However, this wasn't without risk for him.

But moments like this are what we live for. Why battle to stay alive, just to deprive yourself of living? That was often the sentiment expressed to us by the transplant team when asked if certain activities were safe, "You have a second chance at life. Do all the things you want to do while you still can!" We kept the appointment.

The Flight

The flight was all we could think about. Well, that's not entirely fair to say—we thought a lot about Claudia and hoped and prayed for her recovery. But we had something else to think about too.

Something positive. Something that brought us joy. There was an excitement and anticipation that carried us through this otherwise difficult time.

"Never miss an opportunity to do something that brings you joy!" Bradley said to describe our Discovery Flight out of Santa Monica Airport in 2024. We flew with Prometheus Aviation and Captain Max, who let my son do most of the flying. Bradley details our adventure in his chapter of this book.

We arrived at the airport jittery with excitement, meeting the pilot, Max, who would be taking us on this excursion.

It's worth mentioning that a discovery flight is typically an activity performed by a prospective flight student—someone who thinks they may have an interest in flying and wants to try it out. During a discovery flight, with the exception of takeoff and landing, they let *you* fly the plane!

My father urged me to take the captain's seat, insisting that he would get more joy from watching me fly than if he flew himself (he also had a paralyzed arm, which would have made operating the flight controls pretty difficult). At first, I protested, but he was persistent, and eventually, I relented. It wasn't too hard to convince me; I was very excited by the prospect of flying an aircraft!

I looked at the plane and thought, *How the Hell is my dad going to get into the back seat!?* This wasn't a commercial plane with a jet bridge or ladder. You had to climb onto the wing and practically crawl into the tiny doors, which left just enough space for a small adult to enter.

My dad still had very limited cardiac endurance, and the damage from the spinal tumor left his legs weak, his balance poor, his right arm paralyzed, and he had trouble lifting his neck without intense pain. Yet, at this moment, none of that seemed to slow him down in the slightest. With some help from Max and me, he jumped up onto the wing and maneuvered his body into that seat with an agility that seemed to come from a version of himself thirty years younger.

I hopped into the pilot's seat, and we started our preflight checklist.

There was an energy in the cabin as we carried on down the taxiway. That energy surged along with the engines as we turned onto the runway and powered up for takeoff. It's hard to describe the sense of weightlessness you feel in the pit of your stomach as the plane reaches takeoff velocity and starts to lift off the runway. It's the kind of feeling that grounds you in the present moment (pun intended).

After we reached a safe altitude, Max handed over the controls to me.

"Your controls," he said.

"My controls," I confirmed, as he had instructed me to do on the ground.

I placed my left hand on the joystick and my right hand on the throttle.

"Maintain current altitude and start a 360-degree turn to the left," Max instructed.

"Roger," I responded into the mic. That wasn't a word used frequently in my vocabulary, but it seemed appropriate at that moment.

I tilted the joystick to the left, and the plane banked sharply. I noticed our altitude starting to decrease, so I pitched back slightly to maintain lift during the turn. At this point, we were pretty much directly over Venice Beach, and I recognized the breakwater where I had spent so many mornings. The coastline looked gorgeous from up here, and the canyons to our right were breathtaking.

The view from the cockpit during our flight.

"Alright, increase the throttle to seventy percent and climb to 5,000 feet at heading 310," Max instructed.

That seemed like a lot of things to do at once, but my practice in the simulator had prepared me for this moment. My father and I had actually spent hours flying this exact plane in VR, so everything looked somewhat familiar. But in VR, you don't *feel* things.

I pulled back on the joystick a little too hard and felt the G-forces push me down into the seat. I eased off and felt weightless as the aircraft leveled off. This was the part that the simulator couldn't capture—there was nothing else in my mind besides this moment.

I looked back at my dad, who hadn't spoken in some

time. He had a beaming smile, ear to ear, and gave me a thumbs up. These were the moments he fought for. This moment was worth one hundred heart biopsies.

We continued down the coast toward Malibu and made a turn to the northeast when we reached Point Dume. We flew very low over the canyons, so low that I could see the kitchen appliances through the windows of the homes we passed by.

As we made our way toward Van Nuys Airport, we radioed the tower to announce our intentions of a touch-and-go landing. We descended to circuit altitude and entered a right-hand approach pattern. At Max's instruction, I eased back on the throttle, pitched up slightly, and transitioned us into slow flight as we prepared for landing.

"Okay, I'm going to take control back for landing," Max announced.

"My controls."

"Your controls," I responded as I withdrew my hands from the controls.

As Max lowered the flaps, I could feel the angle of attack shift and the aircraft slow as the aerodynamic properties of the wing were altered. I understood more clearly now than ever my father's fascination with aviation. It's hard to express why, but it's the little things like that which sweep away all other thoughts, anchoring you firmly in the present.

We kissed the ground. The moment we touched down was barely perceptible, aside from the brief sound made by the tires as they made contact with the tarmac.

"Flaps set to takeoff, full throttle," Max announced as he configured the controls for the "go" part of our touch-and-go.

The plane lurched forward, and within seconds, we were airborne again. Max brought us back up to a safe altitude and raised the flaps.

"Your controls," he declared.

"My controls," I responded, placing my hands back on the joystick and awaiting his instructions.

"We're going to return to Santa Monica to land," he informed us. "Incidentally, the road you see below us right now, the 405 [freeway], pretty much goes directly to the airport. I want you to maintain the current altitude and airspeed and follow the freeway."

"Got it!" I replied.

"IFR—I Follow the Road," my dad exclaimed from the back seat. This was one of the first times he had spoken the whole flight. He had been silently soaking up the moment, but he couldn't resist telling a bad aviation joke!

This part was really fun. I focused less on the instruments and looked out the window, keeping the freeway just under our left wing. There was a lot of traffic on the

405 (when is there ever not?), but that was of no concern to us as we glided above it.

As we approached the airport, Max took control again. Once again, another butter landing as he safely brought us back down to the ground.

Reflection

That flight had a profound impact on our lives from that moment on. Again, like the wave, it wasn't the flight itself but rather what it represented. It served as a bold reminder of why we endure. It reminded us of the many beautiful experiences in life that give us a reason to keep living.

These moments, like an oasis in the desert, can still be found even during times when life seems to be anything but beautiful. Through this ten-year journey, we learned how easily life can be taken away. There were many friends we made during various hospital stays who, may they rest in peace, were not so lucky and never made it home. Our hearts broke for them and their families.

We carry their memories with us and use them as a daily reminder of the fragility of life—not as a sad reminder, but as a motivating and encouraging one, pushing us to take advantage of our time here on this Earth. Our lives, whether by illness or some freak accident, could end at any moment. We've all become acutely aware of this.

This awareness could be a debilitating and terrifying prospect, and in some respects, it is. But remember, we have the freedom to choose our attitude and how we react to the circumstances that life presents to us. I chose to react by making the most of life and by passionately pursuing all the beautiful experiences it has to offer.

I have joined and participated in various online support groups for transplant recipients and their families. This has been an effort to better understand what my father is going through and to help—and be helped by—family members who are sharing similar experiences.

There was one individual in particular whose story stood out to me. I won't share his name out of respect for his privacy, but he posted something on *Facebook* that resonated deeply. He wrote that his family was worried that he seemed less enthusiastic about life, while the opposite was true. His transplant, he wrote, had given him peace and joy about simply existing and feeling glad to be alive and that was all that mattered.

His post struck a chord with me, because this man had become captivated by the simple pleasure of existence. He had chosen to embrace the joy of being alive, disregarding all the insignificant details that might otherwise cause frustration or fear.

I wish my father had never had to experience any of this, but in a way, I am grateful for having had the opportunity to share this life experience with him. I am still young—at the time of writing this, I'm twenty-nine years old.

This is a revelation and a perspective on life that many people don't gain until much later, and some never do. What a privilege it is to have been given the perspective to see life through this lens. And what a gift it is to still have my father in my life to share in its experiences.

Chapter 4

Why Did I Go to Hell?
My Life Has Been Judged and Found Wanting

By Dr. Rob

For the sake of clarity, this chapter deals with events that occurred in November 2015. These events took place at the second hospital where I was treated after being transferred from the first facility. I was taken by ambulance to the first hospital on October 29, 2015, immediately after the near-fatal head-on collision and STEMI heart attack. I remained at that facility for approximately two weeks.

What follows describes a cardiac arrest and code shortly after a life-saving emergency procedure was performed at the second hospital. I recovered from this first cardiac arrest code despite not being expected to survive due to the extensive, irreversible damage to my heart, which was allowed to occur at the first facility.

These events are described from medical, spiritual, personal, and shared perspectives—mine, my wife's, and my son's and my son-in-law's. During this experience, I went through various states of consciousness and varying degrees of responsiveness.

Love, Life, and a Return from Darkness

The only thing I fully understood upon regaining consciousness after that first horrendous near-cardiac death experience was that it was the sheer force of Claudia's pure love—and God's blessing—that gave me a second chance. Tenuous and shaky as that chance was at the time, it was enough. Perhaps it goes without saying that my love and desire to be with her were equal factors in my return and my desire to have more life with her.

The other thing I fully understood was that I had just returned from that part of the universe that absolutely could not be mistaken for heaven. It was crystal clear—I had gone to Hell.

Imagine trying to process the triple shock:

1. You have just died (Pulseless Ventricular Fibrillation).

2. You realize that you are doomed forever to the absolute darkness, emptiness, coldness, and terror of that river of darkness we call Hell.

3. And then, after all that—you are resuscitated, barely brought back to life!

However, what's even more unusual and distinctive about this is that I regained consciousness long after the resuscitation attempt *failed.* I was basically just sitting on the bed like a plant that was being watered.

A Physician Confronting the Unthinkable

Intellectually, once I regained consciousness, I immediately grasped—as an internal medicine physician—the meaning of two of these things. I had seen them before:

• People going through periods of cardiac arrest and pulseless V-fib.

• Patients coming back during advanced cardiac life support and resuscitation.

Rarely, however, do people come back *long after* these resuscitative attempts have failed.

The third and hardest thing to confront was what appeared to be my final destination.

As I looked at the various IV poles and medications being used to keep me alive artificially, I knew how bleak the immediate outlook was. This realization was compounded by the fact that my ejection fraction, as explained earlier, was only about eleven percent to fifteen percent after the heart attack.

Facing Death While Others Prepared for It

While I was unresponsive, the nursing, respiratory, and cardiology teams had told my wife that I would not survive this. They had advised her to call the kids and have them fly in to see me one last time before, inevitably, pulling the plug after the next cardiac and respiratory failure.

The respiratory therapist had even told Claudia that, in her 16 years of work, she had never seen anyone come back from the point I had reached. She initially refused the cardiologist's order to extubate me because she did not think I would survive.

My wife replied, "I'm glad we made history for you."

None of this is intended to be humorous or flippant—I'm just recording what I was told happened.

The Silent Tug of War Between Life and Death

While unconscious and unresponsive, an intense, silent tug of war between life and death raged for hours. At any second during that struggle, the scales could have tipped toward the darkness and the end—but somehow, I managed to return to the fight. I willed my fading sense of self toward Claudia's voice.

It was a real, actual war where time, precious time, mattered more than ever. It reminded me of a line from Virgil's poem, *Georgics*, where he wrote that time is fleeing and can never be retrieved. Never was that more true than at that moment.

Desperate Measures to Prove I Was Gone

To make clear to my wife that I was unresponsive to pain, they pushed pointed objects up the bottom of my feet, twisted my nipples, and ground their knuckles into my chest. They needed her to accept that I was gone.

(These things may sound barbaric, but they are routine and necessary procedures to establish if there is any response to painful stimuli.)

I consistently did not respond. My pupils were fixed, dilated, and unresponsive to light—another sign that "nobody was home upstairs."

But in the face of all these signs, Claudia never stopped talking to me. She begged me to return and prayed on her knees for me in the ICU.

The Bridge Back to Life

At the end of this first episode—after what felt like an endless push and pull—suddenly, inexplicably, I felt something grasp my rapidly fading sense of self. It pulled me back over the bridge from death and dying.

I returned to Claudia's voice, her hand, her beautiful and exhausted, tearful eyes. I felt horrible pain everywhere. But for now—for an unknown amount of time—I had a second chance at life.

I wasn't gone.

I was ALIVE!

(It sounds better if you say it like Frankenstein would.)

A War Between Pain and Love

Throughout this process of returning from the so-called beyond, I was trapped in a kind of approach-avoidance conflict. The closer I got to Claudia's voice, the more I became aware of increasing physical pain.

Transitioning back from a dying, disembodied entity to a broken, living human being was excruciating. I was tempted and pulled by something malevolent and foreboding to just give up—to let go, take the easy way, and sink back into infinite darkness.

There was a strangely attractive, evil presence trying to influence me into giving up on life. It felt like a powerful telepathic communication from a dark entity forcing itself into my fading sense of self.

That, and for other reasons described elsewhere, is how I knew for certain that I was going to Hell—and absolutely nowhere else.

The Agony of Returning to Life

The closer I got to Claudia's voice, the more aware I became of:

• My broken ribs from the CPR.

• The pain of breathing.

• My damaged teeth from intubation.

• The chest pain from the heart attack.

Worst of all was the realization that I was intubated on a ventilator, with a sensation of drowning, suffocating, and being choked all at the same time.

I tried to imagine the ventilator settings so I could work with them and not struggle against them. Despite my best efforts, I couldn't find the rhythm, and I was overwhelmed with panic at the feeling of being unable to breathe.

Still, none of these agonies were enough to stop me from getting back to my beloved Claudia—and to life itself. I had barely escaped what felt like an eternity of suffering. But for how long?

A Harsh Reality After the Miracle

Every day we had been together since we first met had been an unbelievably charged, happy, love-filled celebration. It almost felt like a party that would never end.

But now, we were slapped in the face with the cold, hard reality that my life—and our existence together—had very nearly ended. Furthermore, what life I had left was hanging by a thread.

The Weight of My Professional Life

In my professional life, I had participated in and led many cardiac arrest and resuscitation codes. I was certified in Advanced Trauma Life Support and Advanced Cardiac Life Support. I was no stranger to death.

Yet, I imagine that at some point, everyone who has ever lived has wanted to deny and defy this reality. I also imagine that most people take it for granted that when they die, they will not find themselves doomed to a river of darkness and suffering for eternity.

But I was alive. Just barely.

Questions of Faith and Judgment

At this point, I was vaguely aware, far from the point where I could rationally attempt to plan the future with all its implications.

I had to consider how this would change Claudia's life, our family's life, our finances, our home—everything. Emails kept coming in. Bills still needed to be paid. It's amazing how quickly one's mind returns to the mundane, even after an earth-shattering experience like this.

But the elephant in the room remained:

Why had I found myself undoubtedly destined for Hell?

My Life Has Been Judged and Found Wanting

Desperate and afraid, I initially turned to the Bible.

How is it possible that I am going to Hell?

I needed a cornerstone of some sort, a starting point of reference to understand what was going on. When my sons were little, I would read from the Bible to them every night until they fell asleep. I'm not sure how much they got out of that, other than the quality time we spent together.

However, I found myself returning to the Bible after reading the entire thing once before. It took me well over a year to do so. Now, at this point in my life, I felt the need to return to the Bible, as I remembered the strength and clarity it had given me when I had read it earlier.

Returning to the concept of curses, I found Deuteronomy 28, which lists curses that would come upon those who did not obey God's commandments. In other words, follow God's commands with a joyful and glad heart, with wholehearted commitment to His laws and commandments—or suffer the consequences, which would be curses. To put it simply, the curses are appropriate to which of God's laws were broken. The punishment fits the crime. I was getting warmer in terms of understanding why I might be sent to Hell.

The heart is often used metaphorically in the Bible to represent the inner self—one's emotions, will, and moral inclinations. In this context, serving God with a joyful and glad heart implies a sincere and wholehearted commitment to His laws and commandments. The absence of such an attitude would result in the curses described in Deuteronomy 28.

I certainly could not honestly say that I had always lived my life with a joyful and glad heart and a wholehearted commitment to His laws and commandments—those being the operative conditions to receive God's rewards and avoid His curses. So, there's that.

More seriously, I think of the patients' lives entrusted to me when I was in training—specifically, the lives that were lost under my care.

Here, then, is some causality as to why I went to Hell.

In theory, there was always a hierarchy—older, more experienced, supervising doctors, residents, attendings, etc.—who were supposedly available in case you needed help. But in real life, when it hits the fan with a patient, sometimes there isn't time to get more people to help because they're all tied up. Especially in an understaffed, inner-city New York hospital like the one where I trained.

What haunts me most are those times when there *were* more people available—even in the middle of the day—but I was just too overwhelmed or too tired to handle those patients' lives as I should have. In those days, I was working thirty-six-hour shifts, every third day, for years at a time. Sometimes those shifts did not end at all and would turn into five days nonstop.

You must consider that these were different times.

His crucifixion frees me from being bound by the Old Testament rules and the guarantee of Hell for what were unforgivable sins prior to Jesus' dying on the cross for our sins.

For the first time in my life, I now understand what this actually means. I finally understand the difference between the Old Testament and the New Testament—the covenant of Abraham and the covenant with Jesus.

Jesus literally suffered the torture, pain, shame, and humiliation of crucifixion for me, personally—and for any-one else who will accept Him as their personal savior. *This* is what it actually means to have a personal relationship with Jesus Christ. I never even remotely grasped that before.

Nonetheless, not *honoring thy mother and thy father* to the degree that I did still leaves one with a pretty embedded and distinctly damned feeling. Literally.

It is still a mortal sin.

What I Did, What I Didn't Do, and What I Could Have Done

My father, immediately after divorcing my mother, left for Brazil, where he was from. His family was German and had left for Brazil at the time of World War II. He allegedly fled to avoid paying child support and alimony. I had very little contact with him after he left—I was about six or seven at the time.

My mother's father, my grandfather, Armando, was an amazing man. He stepped in and did all he could to be a father to me.

He was a judge in Poland and had to flee to Brazil from the Nazis. Every weekend, he would do something special and adventurous with me. For example, he would take me out to Riverside, California, where we could take glider rides. When I was fifteen and a half and got my learner's permit, he bought me a motorcycle. Or we would go to the marinas and investigate boats that were for sale. We would always manage to have the dealership take us out for a spin.

I guess that's where I got my inspiration for doing the same types of things with my sons as they were growing up. I know what a massive impact that made on my life, and I wanted to share those joys of living with my sons.

My biological father, in contrast, would occasionally return to California. On the way to the airport to return to Brazil, he would call to say he was stopping by to give me a gift and would leave it on our backyard doorstep. Sometimes, he wouldn't stay to speak with me at all. He was afraid of the legal consequences of not having paid child support and alimony.

It's funny, because at that time, my mother worked for a Brazilian airline, Varig. Other employees of the airline would always notify her when my father's name appeared on one of the flight manifests. She always knew he was in town, but she never did anything to enforce the court-ordered settlement agreement.

After completing my internal medicine residency at Mt. Sinai in New York, I was recruited and moved to California by Kaiser Permanente, Southern California Medical Group, where I worked for about three years. I was then recruited by a major hospital corporation (Columbia) and moved to Florida in 1993, the year of Hurricane Andrew.

The very first week I arrived in Florida, with my first wife, my father showed up unexpectedly and unannounced at my door.

We had just moved into our condo, with boxes everywhere. We hadn't even begun to get organized after this huge move. He had with him his beautiful daughter from his common-law marriage in Brazil. I had no idea how he found me or knew what my new address was.

Out of the clear blue sky, he asked me to take his eighteen-year-old daughter in, put her through college, and basically take care of her until she got on her feet and had her life together. I had never even met her before! I'm not a hundred percent sure I had heard anything about her before this. I was flabbergasted and confused.

I didn't realize at the time that he had literally spent his last dollar on the trip to try to see me and get help for himself and his daughter. He didn't have two dimes to rub together. Of course, he didn't tell me any of that at the time. Nor did he come out and tell me that he was a dying man.

Nevertheless, I felt all along during that brief one-week visit that something was very off and wrong, but I did not pursue it to find out what it was. He was staying at the cheapest motels possible and certainly didn't look like he was well off or anything.

Needless to say, my ex-wife was not thrilled about this situation, and my mother, when I told her what was happening, was furious at the request after the way she had been treated. She had been forced to work two jobs to support me, etc. This, after he had basically fled the country to avoid paying child support and alimony.

I was very strongly influenced by my mother, whom I love deeply. Both of us had moved here from Brazil, and her going through a divorce, being a single parent and enduring other hardships made us very close. If I had been more of a man, more independent, and a real son to my father and less influenced by my ex-wife and immediate family around me, no matter what, things would've ended differently.

Much later, while Claudia and I were moving from one home to another, I would find bundles and bundles of letters that my father had written to me, which I did not recall having seen. I started reading some, but was so overwhelmed with sadness and loss that I have been unable to finish reading them. They are just too painful.

I also found out much later, from his granddaughter, who is my niece, that he was the kind of man who, if he had two shirts, would give one away if someone else was shirtless.

Like I said, I had just arrived in Florida, just months before Hurricane Andrew hit. I was just starting to get oriented and hadn't even begun seeing patients yet. The hospital corporation that had recruited me (Columbia Pompano Beach Medical Center) had given me a sign-on bonus and paid for my move, but at that point, I had no real income yet.

I guess I'm not much of a detective, but looking back on this, I should've asked myself the obvious question: *Why would a man do something like this, something so desperate?*

To make matters worse, in terms of my lack of perception, curiosity, or even basic common human decency: A few months before my move, I had started receiving emails from my father. He was asking questions about treatment for prostate cancer and possible brain tumors, etc. I gave him the appropriate medical information by way of answering him. But I failed to realize that he had absolutely no access to any kind of decent medical care. My heart was turned away from him, and I didn't have eyes to see or ears to hear what he was really telling me.

The irony is squirm-worthy. I was diagnosed with prostate cancer and received five intensive radiation treatments, also at UCLA. In September 2023, I was diagnosed with a spinal tumor, which caused a fall and a hip fracture in August 2023.

The following year, my heart transplant occurred on February 15, 2024. My history of prostate cancer and a spinal tumor, which was at the base of my brain, almost disqualified me as a candidate for a heart transplant.

These two conditions, both of which my father had, unbeknownst to me, had led to his death. Granted, his brain tumor was a slightly different type, but nonetheless, we both had extremely similar conditions, except he did not survive his. Without me he didn't stand a chance—and I wasn't there for him.

At the time when he came to see me, I was probably the one and only person in the world who could have saved his life by simply admitting him to the hospital that had recruited me. I could easily have ordered all the appropriate tests and consults, and I could've gotten him more than adequate treatment, and he might still be alive today.

I turned my back on my own father at a time of life-or-death crisis. I was the one person who could've helped him—saved him, literally—and I let him walk away and go to his death after coldly turning my back on him.

It wasn't until ten years after he had passed away that I learned of his death.

To make matters worse, when I asked about where he was buried, I found out from his daughter, who had contacted my sons, that he was buried in a mass grave with no marker, in a small village on the seaside in Brazil. In other words, he was buried in the town garbage pit.

Honor thy father and thy mother? Apparently not me.

This, I think, is my unforgivable, mortal sin, and fatal life failing. This is why I say, with conviction and certainty, my life has been judged and found wanting. This is why I am cursed to go to Hell, and then paradoxically blessed to return a total of ten times so far.

Please, Lord, forgive me for this and spare me from the horrible, terrifying, endless darkness when the final time comes. Please, Lord, let me be with my beloved Claudia and family when my race is run.

Chapter 5

Why Did My Husband Go to Hell?

By Claudia Treuherz

I've pondered why Robert went to Hell, and why, immediately following his cardiac death, he kept saying, "I have been judged and found wanting."

I didn't quite understand this because I knew him as a good man and a "decent" Catholic. He most certainly knew and acknowledged Jesus Christ. *Was that not enough?* I knew the answer to that, but denial was so much easier.

The one obvious reason I could think of as to why he ended up in Hell was because he truly did not have a relationship with God and Jesus. The not-so-obvious reason was the simple fact that Robert carried a small cemetery in his brain. He blamed himself for the death of so many people, his father included. He remembered the name of each patient he had lost. He was tortured by the idea that he hadn't done enough. He wondered if, maybe, if he had done this or that, the terminally ill patients might have lived longer.

He never had any power over death, no matter how good of a doctor he was. All these matters were absolutely out of his control, but he mulled over them, torturing himself as if he were God, as if somehow, he could have changed the outcome. His guilt overwhelmed him and kept him at arm's length from God's abundant mercy and love. He was his own worst enemy.

When he finally realized that God is in control, not him, he surrendered and accepted the love and grace that was given to him. For the first time in his life, he understood that he was not the one in control—God was.

Our days are not guaranteed; they are to be appreciated and celebrated each day. Every morning, I wake up and I thank God for allowing me to live another day, knowing very well that tomorrow is not within my control. I do not worry about it. I let God lead the day. I still make plans, but I pray about them. I pray that God's will be done, not my own.

Indeed, making plans and talking about the future has never been more fun. Hoping my plans align with God's plan is not easy, but I do not despair or get frustrated when my plans are blown out of the water. I've learned that my best plans and dreams were garbage compared to what God has in store for me instead. The saying, "If God closes a door, He always opens a window," is incorrect. When God closes a door, He removes a wall, builds a large barn door, and brings a G6 luxury private jet for your transport. All that is needed is faith.

Since the transplant (Rob's G6), he has been consumed with "tomorrow." Not in the way you might imagine. He's consumed with what we should do for our next vacation—go to Hawaii, spend time with our children and grandchildren, explore New Zealand, see Japan, cruise to Alaska, buy a boat, repair old heirloom jewelry to leave to our children, move to Florida, and so much more. Suddenly, our world has opened up. We have so much to do, so much to see, and so much to accomplish—so much to live for.

I am looking forward to our first post-transplant vacation. May God bless and watch over all of you.

Chapter 6

Picking Up the Pieces

By Dr. Rob

The picture below is what I looked like approximately four weeks after the heart attack and car accident, on the day of my discharge from the second hospital facility, which was the eve of Thanksgiving 2015. The accident had occurred on October 29, 2015. This photo shows a sharp contrast to how I looked in photos that were taken weeks and months before the heart attack.

Four weeks after the car accident, heart attack, and first near-death experience.

Or, to put it another way, here I sat, brokenhearted. I had come to finish but realized I was only just getting started.

So, at that point, there I was—about four weeks from the original car accident that occurred on October 29th, 2015—sitting in the second hospital since the accident and about a week and a half from the first sudden cardiac near-death experience. Out of an abundance of caution, the cardiologist decided to perform a second angiogram prior to discharging me. This was to make absolutely sure there were no further or additional blockages in any of the coronary arteries that could result in further infarct or myocardial cell death just before discharging me home.

That second angiogram showed nothing new, and I was discharged home with the plan to start outpatient cardiac rehabilitation and maintain close follow-up with this cardiologist.

It should be mentioned that, at this point, I had not yet been placed with an implanted defibrillator or pacemaker, which would protect me from any episodes of ventricular tachycardia or ventricular fibrillation.

The temporary solution was something called a LifeVest. This medieval-looking device is an externally worn, battery-powered set of electrodes that are prepared to shock you at any time should you go into ventricular fibrillation, ventricular tachycardia, or any of the other malignant rapid irregular heart rates. It is an extraordinarily uncomfortable device, to say the least.

The scariest part of this is that it must be removed for me to take a shower. So, during those ten minutes or so in the shower, I stood there in suspense, not knowing if I might drop dead at any moment.

Also, we were only provided with one such device, which meant that my shower was the only opportunity to clean this garment and dry it at the same time, so it would be ready to be put on immediately after.

We were told in no uncertain terms—and I understood as a doctor—that the chances of a spontaneous fatal cardiac arrhythmia were a virtual certainty.

I was able to stop wearing the LifeVest in January 2016 when a defibrillator was implanted in my chest. Boy, did it get a workout! It saved me many times, although it's not possible to think of a more unpleasant form of salvation.

As if all this weren't enough, another axiom or words of wisdom born of experience that I would share with my sons and wife about medicine and heart attack/cardiac patients in general was, "If the heart attack doesn't kill them, the pneumonia will."

So, about this time—around one and a half weeks after discharge from the second hospital facility (see picture at the beginning of this chapter), where I coded and had that horrible first NDE—I started coughing. Really coughing. Within forty-eight hours, I had developed a productive cough (meaning one can cough up mucus) with a high fever of 102.5.

I called the pulmonary doctor who had been treating me after my code, and he readmitted me to the facility I had just been discharged from. He started treating me for post-intubation pneumonia, which meant the process of being put on a ventilator and intubated had resulted—as it commonly does—in a serious pneumonia.

Ironically, this was exactly the kind of situation I had been describing to my wife and sons. So, of course, this turned into a life-threatening situation and actually required a bronchoscopy and bronchial lavage because I was too weak to cough effectively and clear the infected secretions that were drowning me as they overwhelmed my immune system with infected pulmonary material.

This meant a tube was inserted into my lungs (three lobes on the right and two on the left) and antibiotics and mucus-clearing liquids were used to flush out the infected materials. This ghastly procedure is done while conscious because it is necessary to cough while this is going on to help clear out the toxic materials in the lungs.

Normally, family members are absolutely *not* allowed while this procedure is happening, but Claudia would not take no for an answer. She insisted on being at my side throughout, holding my hand, and being there with me.

This is not a pleasant procedure to watch or have done to you. But it saved my life and cleaned out my lungs enough to allow the IV antibiotics and inhaled breathing treatments to work.

It's not at all unusual for heart attack patients to succumb to this kind of pneumonia, but once again, God and Claudia would not allow this to happen. I survived this pneumonia, and after about two weeks, I was discharged home. Weaker and thinner, I realized that I had seen many corpses that looked better than I did at that point in time.

Nonetheless, at about this time, I entered traditional cardiac rehabilitation to strengthen my heart and my overall physical strength. This was a program affiliated with the hospital where one exercises under supervised care. And theoretically, gradually, the patient improves with time.

Unfortunately, in my case, the damage to my heart was so extensive that I had what was called a paradoxical response to exercise. Instead of my heart rate increasing or my blood pressure rising in response to exercise, it would drop or crash to unsafe levels, making me feel sick, scared, and unable to continue.

Needless to say, this was not a good prognostic sign. The fact that my heart was so damaged that it would not respond to gentle exercise to improve its function was a devastating prognostic indicator.

Simultaneously, in the background, normal life had not ceased. There were still bills to be paid, questions of future financial planning, and the issue of whether I would be able to maintain working and producing an income—all of which were very stressful. These were important questions to think about and plan for, and we were dealing with all of this simultaneously while just trying to keep me alive.

Our cardiologist at the time, who had saved my life after the failure at the first facility and whom I hold in very high esteem, decided to refer me to UCLA's heart transplant program for an evaluation.

The general level of people's awareness of what is involved in an actual heart transplant, and to my surprise, this extended to me even as a physician, only represented the bottommost part of a very steep learning curve.

The evaluation process itself, to qualify for a heart transplant, is unbelievably complex and involved and takes a couple of weeks. It requires being admitted—I was in 2017—to UCLA for an open-heart transplant evaluation.

This comprehensive evaluation for a transplant patient's candidacy involves every field of medicine, including psychiatry, dermatology, orthopedics, urology, and gastroenterology. The patient is also screened for drug abuse. They are not going to invest in a new heart for you if you're going to die of colon cancer or prostate cancer or not take your anti-rejection medications, rendering the transplant useless.

Interestingly, this also involves a thorough and deep dive into your finances and immediate family and support structure. (Insurance doesn't cover everything—especially medications.)

Many candidates for heart transplants are rejected because their family support structure fails to meet their strict criteria. Imagine the terrible dilemma: *you DON'T qualify for a heart transplant because you DON'T have any dedicated, committed family or friends.*

This is because the medical team knows that the post-transplant process is so demanding for nearly a year that one must have committed family members—at least two at all times (who have to actually sign a contract with UCLA)—willing to be present 24/7 for months at a time to take you to numerous follow-up visits per week at UCLA, which can take the entire day (and usually do).

This includes sudden unexpected admissions for complications and calls at any time, day or night, from the transplant coordinators instructing you to go to the hospital for another heart biopsy or invasive (meaning a central line is needed to receive the treatment in question) infusion of anti-rejection medications, or for a series of treatments called plasmapheresis, which are similar to dialysis as they remove from the blood anti-bodies that could cause rejection of the heart.

There are constant medication adjustments requir-ing innumerable visits to the UCLA pharmacy and lab at early morning hours, and sudden, nearly frantic calls from UCLA telling you that you must be readmitted immediately because of something discovered in your most recent lab work dealing with rejection issues.

This process is not for the faint-hearted. It is a very long-term process and commitment. It is committing one-self, if you are blessed enough to receive a heart at all, to setting your life on a new trajectory—a trajectory towards what they refer to as a new normal. This is because, from the moment you receive a transplanted organ, your body busily sets about doing its best to reject it.

The UCLA transplant team, with their unbelievable and nationwide unbeatable track record of success in managing complex issues surrounding rejection, stands ready and makes sure that you are standing ready as well to do whatever it takes to make sure that you honor and sustain and do not reject this heart.

So, I went through this incredibly involved process and qualified. Remember, this was still in 2017—or, in other words, the first time I went through the open-heart transplant evaluation process and qualified. The second time was in January/February 2024, and I received the heart transplant on Valentine's Day (the process started on Valentine's Day but required a couple of days for completion).

I was about to be "listed" on UNOS—the United Network for Organ Sharing—when one of the doctors, Dr. Baas, came into the room at the end of the evaluation and said to me and Claudia, "Rob, there is one more thing you can do."

You see, Dr. Baas understood, probably better than anyone, that qualifying for a heart transplant was one thing, while receiving a heart was something else, and then keeping it from being rejected was still yet another thing.

One more component to this, one that is not well appreciated, is that the average life expectancy after a heart transplant is eight years. Eight years! Of course, there's wide variability in this figure depending on how compliant the patient is with his or her post-transplant medication regimen, which is extremely complex.

Therefore, you want to receive your transplanted heart as late as possible, since it comes with a kind of "expiration date."

Generally speaking, the age cutoff for a heart transplant is somewhere in the early seventies, although this is not written in stone. In other words, you want to get your first heart transplant before your early- to mid-seventies because you're not likely to get another one after that.

Further complicating the situation is that if you wait too late, you might die from complications of the heart disease, which made you qualify for the heart transplant in the first place. Which is exactly what almost happened to me.

There are people who have lived thirty years with a heart transplant, and I am going to be one of them!

So, this one more thing that Dr. Baas was referring to: It meant enrolling in UCLA's "cardiac reversal program." This is an involved lifestyle modification program that includes, among other things, extensive nutritional counseling.

In other words, basically relearning how to eat, read labels, shop for food, etc. Also, exercising under strict supervised conditions, even while having chest pain, to force one's heart to improve—which required a lot of courage on my part.

This program required participation twice a week, four-and-a-half hours a day for nine weeks. Imagine the disruption to any schedule this would cause, given that we had a very long drive in both directions. This was nothing compared to what would come later during the actual transplant period when they required that we live within a certain distance. My son Bradley left his apartment in Seattle, drove down to LA and relocated for those four months to this Airbnb to be physically present 24/7 for that period, as required byUCLA as the second "primary" caretaker.

This cardiac reversal program included a stress management component, yoga, group therapy, and relaxation training—basically an incredible commitment to do whatever it takes to make the heart that God gave you last as long as possible.

An unexpected "side effect" or benefit of this program was that it kept us so busy between driving, shopping, and figuring out how to live and cook and eat, that we didn't have time to be depressed or worried or focus too much on what was still going on with my heart or what had to, and would, inevitably, happen and what had already happened.

Frankly, I was very skeptical about the probability of success with this program. Particularly when I heard about things like stress management and yoga and group therapy, something I had had little experience with. Funny, but I was never taught anything about nutrition in medical school, let alone how to read a food label or shop for healthy foods.

To my surprise and shock, all of this worked better than I could have ever imagined! I went from weighing 220 pounds to 160 in less than a year.

We achieved this mainly (only, really) due to the commitment, enthusiasm and sheer force of will and Love of Claudia. This program can only work if you and your partner are one hundred percent committed to stick to it together and turn away from distractions and temptation.

We stuck to this program like white on rice for years to make my existing heart last almost nine years longer. The program and the lifestyle changes we made to conform to it were key to that success. This was not an easy program. The foods were not commonly available. We had to shop at specialty grocery stores such as Whole Foods or Sprouts to get what we needed.

It was especially difficult for us, as we live almost two hours from UCLA, and there are no Whole Foods or Sprouts markets near us. So, we had the double whammy of long drives to and from UCLA and the markets. These foods are also more expensive than the lower-quality, higher-fat options that are readily available.

One of the key rules was that we could buy nothing with more than three grams of fat. Sounds easy, right? Try going to a market and reading every label. It was a painstaking process.

Claudia also had to learn to cook with no butter and no oil. Imagine trying to cook without those staples. And the sole source of protein was beans and tofu. This diet meant no meat, no fish, no sushi—only plant-based protein. Can you imagine how difficult eating out at almost any restaurant was?

Unbelievably, Claudia managed to find ways to make tofu taste good. So, we lived like this for years, which gave us the time we needed to wait for a delayed, life-prolonging transplant.

This challenging but effective program worked until my heart could take no more. It started to fail quickly, just before the transplant, which I was fortunate enough to live long enough to receive. So, that "one more thing" bought us almost ten more years before the transplant—years fraught with frightening, unexpected complications and nine more near-death experiences along the way.

Chapter 7

The Blessing of My Father-in-Law

By Alan Davenport

At the time of the accident, I was not yet a part of the family. That would not happen until after I met Claudia's beautiful daughter, Amber, on May 9th, 2019.

Right off the bat, we fell in love. Without wasting any time, we moved into a home together in August of 2019. Amber and I were drunk in love, and I can still smell her perfume from the first night we met. On March 19th, 2022, we got married, and from that day forward, I became a part of this amazing family.

Amber and Alan on their wedding day, March 19th, 2022.

I was welcomed into the family with open arms, and I am so grateful to have each and every one of them in my life. I am a firm believer that every person who comes across our path in life has a divine purpose and reason behind it. Dr. Rob Treuherz has, without a doubt, had a big impact on my life in many ways.

Out of everyone in the family, I would have never thought that Dr. Rob and I would have developed the bond that we have today. I am so thrilled to have come across this unexpected relationship with a fellow "brother in Christ," as I like to say. Whenever we start a conversation and catch up on our time apart, we hardly waste a single second talking about anything that is surface level or lacks deep meaning.

What's strange is that our upbringings, career paths, and life experiences are almost total opposites. Dr. Rob completed one of the most difficult college paths one could pursue in becoming a doctor, while I am a college dropout. Dr. Rob has class and speaks multiple languages, whereas I prefer to wear sweatpants and t-shirts in any setting. I live in Miami and can hardly speak a lick of Spanish (let alone any other languages). Rob spent his high school years in the Los Angeles area, while I spent mine in Kansas City, Missouri.

With all these differences, you would assume that we may not see eye to eye, but contrary to that, it's quite the opposite. As I said earlier, I believe that everyone who crosses your path in life has a reason and purpose. Then I stop to think about Dr. Rob and his slim chances of surviving everything he's been through. The fact that he is alive today to share with me his life experiences, his faith in Christ, his struggles, and successes, strengthens my belief that every word we share together is THAT much more meaningful.

I feel very strongly that God has not only spared his life so that he may live in the land for his repentance of his sins, but that God has also spared his life so that he was able to live long enough to cross my path. Through our time together and the words we share, I can inherit something of value—experiences and lessons that I can pass along to my daughter and the next generation.

Let's go back to January 2nd, 2024. The day that changed everything and ultimately led to Dr. Rob's open heart transplant surgery. Unlike Bradley's day, where he mentioned that his day was going great, my day was stressful and hectic, filled with uncertainties about the short term and, quite frankly, the long term. The holidays were over, and it was time to get back to work. Amber and I were staying with Robert and Claudia at their beautiful Florida home while they were in town for the holidays.

Before I dive in further, I want to give some context. Our daughter was born on October 12th, 2023, so at the time, I was new to being a father, still learning the ropes. Here are two pictures of our beautiful daughter, Alaia:

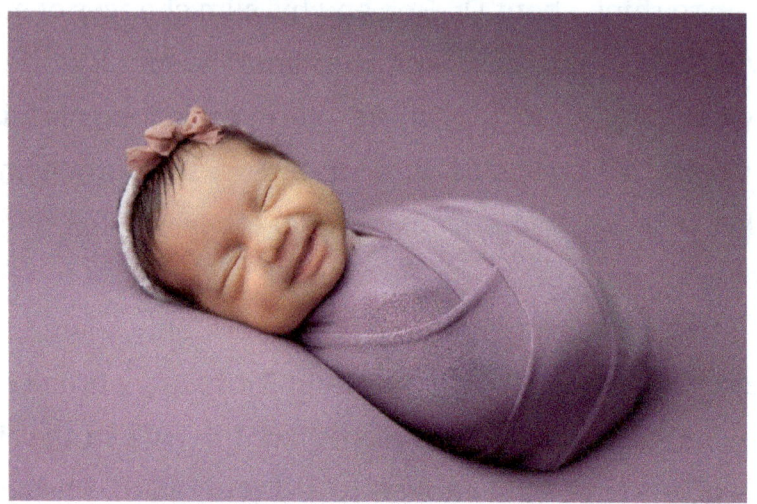

Beautiful baby Alaia.

As beautiful as this part of life was, it was also stressful (although Claudia made it much easier on Amber and me while she was visiting). My bread-and-butter business wasn't doing well. My business partner and I had to stop payroll during this time. Needless to say, having your first baby the same month you cut payroll for the first time in over a decade is terrifying. I was living on my savings, and by the grace of God, I had some.

With Claudia being there to help, I could start the day by answering work emails and figuring out where a missing shipment was for my jewelry business. As I mentioned earlier, the business was in a rough spot. I was also trying to fix over 300 incorrect orders, as our solid gold manufacturer had mispacked them. After handling the jewelry work, I ran errands and restocked items for our two Airbnbs.

Then, I received an email from our jewelry supplier saying they couldn't find the missing shipment and didn't have a tracking number. This never happens. As the COO of our business, this responsibility falls on me, and I didn't know what to do. I was stressed and, honestly, in a bad mood, feeling like everything was crumbling.

As I was driving back from running errands, I saw a fire truck and let it cut in front of me. I thought nothing of it. The fire truck took a turn I had to make, so I followed. It took another turn, and once again, it was the same turn I needed to make. When it turned down the last road I needed, I thought, "I sure hope that fire truck isn't going to their house!"

It was a long road with many other options, but eventually, the worst-case scenario happened: they turned into Dr. Rob and Claudia's neighborhood. I couldn't believe it. I thought maybe there was a small fire and everyone was safe. But before I could park, an ambulance sped onto the scene. People jumped out with a stretcher and ran into the house. The idea of a small fire disappeared, and I knew it had something to do with Dr. Rob's health. I started praying that everything would be okay.

I went inside and found out that Dr. Rob had fallen due to V-tach. Thankfully, his defibrillator shocked him back to life. The girls were panicked, but Dr. Rob seemed in good spirits, almost as if nothing serious had happened. One thing I know about Dr. Rob is that he has a great poker face in the midst of adversity. Maybe, from his perspective, when you've been on the verge of death, nothing in this physical life seems that serious.

Dr. Rob was taken to the hospital, and that day marked the beginning of his road to open heart transplant surgery. The chaos at the house calmed down, and I noticed that I wasn't stressed about the missing shipment or the business anymore. Dr. Rob's life was at risk AGAIN, and that day could have been the end of the road for him. Witnessing everything that happened changed me. Hearing about health scares over the phone is different from seeing them firsthand.

That day, I may not have had a smooth outlook, I may not have had money coming in, and I still didn't have a tracking number for the shipment. But I had my health, a beautiful wife and daughter, and a supportive family. Sometimes life reminds you that your health is your most valuable asset. I believe God sometimes uses someone else's worst day to show others what the true meaning of a "worst day" is.

Like a Father to Me

My biological father and I have not had the best relationship. We don't "hate" or even "dislike" each other. I was never abused physically or verbally. I just think I was an "accident" in his life. Conceived when both parents were 19, they had no plans to have a baby. I think the only reason I wasn't aborted was due to both parents coming from Christian families who didn't believe in abortion.

I love my biological father, and I know deep down he loves me too, but he's never reached out. He didn't come to my high school graduation or wedding, and

I've even offered to buy him plane tickets. I've forgiven him and hold no grudges. We are simply opposites. I am forever grateful to both my parents and grandparents, and to God, for my life.

I share this context because, with the absence of my biological father, Dr. Rob has become a father figure in my life. Despite multiple health scares, Dr. Rob has traveled from Los Angeles to visit us many times. Whenever we catch up, we dive deep into meaningful conversations, often wandering off from others to keep the conversation going.

For some reason, I feel very comfortable speaking with Dr. Rob. I ask him deep, below-the-surface questions that I wouldn't usually ask. I admire his life, perseverance, and ability to overcome intense adversity. I don't know anyone else who has had to persevere the way he has. His accomplishments aren't just about success but overcoming big failures, wrongdoings, and sins.

Sadly, some men allow life's bad things to define them, and the weight of negative situations crushes their spirit. I feel this may be the case with my father. I am going through a phase in my life where I could allow it to weaken me, but I fight against it every day. I remind myself of the Lord's promises and how, no matter how painful, God has always carried me to better situations. There are two spirits at play in this world: God and the devil. I continue to pray for my father, hoping he hasn't let life's negativity define him.

Meanwhile, I draw close to men like Dr. Rob, who has looked death in the eye multiple times. He acknowledged his wrongdoings, repented, and found forgiveness through Jesus Christ. Dr. Rob had his heart removed and replaced with a new one. If he had allowed life's negativity to define him, I don't think he'd have made it this far.

This is why I feel comfortable asking Dr. Rob the deep questions. I don't care about tiptoeing around what I want to know. When you cross paths with someone like Dr. Rob, you must learn as much as you can from a fellow "brother in Christ." He's overcome so much, and his spirit hasn't been crushed. This is why he's a father figure in my life and why I aspire to be like him.

Dr. Rob and Claudia have not only instilled wisdom in me but also made life-altering financial decisions that have helped Amber and me be comfortable. I've met people who talk but never follow through. Dr. Rob and Claudia always keep their word. Because of them, Amber and I were able to have an incredible wedding on a rooftop overlooking Biscayne Bay in Miami.

Wedding day joy for Amber and Alan after the rooftop ceremony overlooking Biscayne Bay in Miami.

When we found out that Amber was pregnant in 2023, Dr. Rob and Claudia helped with the down payment for a larger apartment, as we were living in a one-bedroom apartment at the time. I am forever grateful for this financial assistance. Here is a picture of the view from our new apartment:

The balcony view of Biscayne Bay from the Miami apartment that Amber, Alan, and Alaia call home.

Their generosity has inspired me to work hard, and God willing, I will one day be in a position where I can help my children in the same way.

As I wrap up my chapter, I think it's important to share the day I first started reading this book. Amber and I were in town visiting Dr. Rob for the first time since his heart transplant surgery. This was a week-long stay during the summer of 2024. Dr. Rob had been urging me to read the book, and I kept saying, "I'd love to; I will before I leave." A few days went by, and he asked me again. I made the same claim that I would eventually.

It's not that I didn't want to read it—the trip was packed with activities, and I was also working a little on my laptop every day. The day before we were set to leave, he asked once more. All the activities were done, and the timing was perfect. I finally started reading, and I was instantly hooked!

Before reading, I wasn't aware of the details surrounding the car accident and the following days. Dr. Rob and I sat on his bed, hanging out while I read page by page, asking him questions along the way. Hours flew by, and we took a break for dinner. Afterward, we went back upstairs so I could continue reading. He stayed with me, answering any questions I had.

It was a nice bonding time, almost as if we had been lifetime best friends, with no thirty-four-year age gap between us. It was a day I don't think either of us will forget. A couple of hours passed, and we were approaching 11:00 p.m. Amber called and asked when I would be coming to bed. Dr. Rob encouraged me to read two more pages near the end of the book.

As I scrolled, something caught my eye. I don't even know what it was, but I kept scrolling and read the two pages Rob wanted me to read. Right after finishing those last two pages, I was about to call it a night. But then, I randomly thought, "Let me scroll up and see what caught my eye."

What caught my eye was this, which Dr. Rob had written:

"Granted, I am a Catholic/Christian, and therefore, bound by the New Testament. Meaning sincerely repenting to Jesus and asking for forgiveness of this sin frees me from being bound by the Old Testament rules and guarantees of Hell for what were unforgivable sins prior to Jesus' dying on the cross for our sins."

Let me give some context here. I've believed in my heart that Jesus Christ died on the cross for our sins for decades (I'm thirty-four now). However, I admit that I didn't truly understand the meaning of Jesus' sacrifice or the difference between the Old and New Testament until I read Dr. Rob's words.

I believed it, but I wondered for decades about the deeper meaning. Those two sentences made everything click. I had never really thought about the world before Jesus—riddled with sin and in desperate need of a Savior. God was not a physical man on Earth back then. It must have been so much harder to believe!

Sin was rampant. But God "loved the world so much that he gave his only Son, that whoever believes in him shall not perish but have eternal life," according to John 3:16. So Jesus was sent! He, God in human form, fulfilled all the Old Testament prophecies. His death and resurrection reset the clock on time. We often forget that the current year is 2024 AD. AD stands for "Anno Domini" meaning "in the year of the Lord," not After Death. It is meant to be the year Jesus was born. And Christmas isn't about presents, just as Easter isn't about Easter eggs or bunny rabbits.

I understand that some readers may not believe these things, and I'm not trying to force my beliefs on anyone. But for anyone curious or on the fence, I encourage you to try reading the Bible with an open heart. When I finished reading, I looked at Dr. Rob and asked, "If all of these things had never happened to you, where would you be spiritually?"

He replied, "I would be spiritually dead." It was a powerful moment.

A few days later, I came across this scripture in the Book of Job (33:28-30): "God has delivered me from going down to the pit, and I shall live to enjoy the light of life. God does all these things to a person—twice, even three times—to turn them back from the pit, that the light of life may shine on them."

Dr. Rob's life is a modern-day story similar to Job's in many ways. Unfortunately, God has tested Dr. Rob more than three times. But is it really "unfortunate"? Or were these events divinely designed to save him from the pit of Hell—the very pit he fell into before coming back to life?

To me, a big reason Dr. Rob's life has been spared over and over is so that he could write this book. I believe it will help and encourage many people in countless ways, not just in the short term, but for generations to come.

After reading, my entire perspective on life changed. Thank you, Dr. Rob, for giving me the opportunity to have a chapter in this book. It is truly an honor.

Chapter 8

Nine More Second Chances Culminating in the Heart Transplant

By Dr. Rob

This is probably the most difficult chapter I must write. Reliving these horrors is so intense and unpleasant that it causes me such anxiety and stress that I'm not sure I should even write this. I fear it may be detrimental to my mental health and wellbeing.

However, I've made a commitment to do so, and so I shall.

The mounting PTSD, disorientation, and survival insecurity that followed each of these events are almost impossible to describe. We gave up trying to explain it to people, other than in very general terms. The draining, endless, pointless questions that invariably followed only wore us out more.

No one, except immediate family—and even then, they couldn't really follow the complex issues without formal medical training. As Amber learned when she saw me receive a defibrillator shock, one actually had to witness this to fully grasp its reality.

What's more nebulous and harder to describe is the mounting ennui that builds more and more after each such event.

Without the support of the personnel at UCLA and the literature we turned to for understanding, counseling, and survival tools, I don't think our sanity would have survived.

World-renowned professors such as Dr. Mario C. Deng at UCLA, took time to calm and stabilize Claudia and me mentally after events like these. They made all the difference in the world.

After dropping dead again and again, followed by harrowing drives to the hospital and frightening evaluations with no certainty or encouragement of a longer life, it was the wisdom, experience, and insight of these wise men that carried us through.

Dr. Deng practically hypnotized the two of us in a moment of crisis, leading us into a hyper-focused state of literal time distortion. So intense was his guidance that we learned to call it a "NOW" moment. This was an awareness and laser focus on the power of the present moment, perpetuating and immortalizing the soul-linked love that Claudia and I share.

By "finding" and working every day to evolve our understanding of the "now," we learned that whatever happens—even if one or both of us are separated by death—the NOW moment will go on forever. It's something we can always hold onto, a tactile connection to our lives together, timelessly.

Viktor Frankl, in his 1946 book chronicling his experiences as a concentration camp prisoner, had a central message to say yes to life and discover meaning in life's most difficult experiences. He also emphasized that by consciously visualizing what gives your life meaning, you can tolerate and get through anything, fighting for more time with what truly matters.

Similarly, Eckhart Tolle, in his book, *The Power of Now* (1997), also stresses the importance of living in the present moment. Most of our emotional problems stem from identifying with our minds and dwelling on the past or worrying about the future. He asserts that only the present moment is real and that the past is a construct of the mind.

These ideas convey timeless and empowering thoughts. I share them so that you, too, can hold onto life even when it's being ripped from your hands.

One PTSD therapist gave me and Claudia a valuable tool for dealing with repeated NDEs. She advised, "Ask yourself, are you likely to die *right now*?"

Usually, the answer is *no*, and simply stating this to ourselves was, and is, very calming. We even find ourselves laughing about the intensity of some of these situations. In these NDE moments, after the immediate crisis has passed, we often find ourselves laughing and crying simultaneously at the absurdity and unlikeliness of what we've just survived.

Having procrastinated enough, albeit with good reason, I now move onto the other reality-rocking near-death experiences and battles of life and death:

I've already discussed the first and worst NDE—the one that occurred in 2015, about three weeks after the car accident at the second hospital where I was treated, and shortly after a procedure to repair the failed stents placed incorrectly at the first facility.

For reasons I've already touched on (the attitude of the senior attending cardiologist, which was passed down through the treating team), had that first inevitable NDE occurred at the first facility, I would have died right there and then. I would have died in November 2015. Instead, it's now August 2024, and I'm sixteen months into my new life after a heart transplant!

That first experience was the worst for so many reasons: the clear vision of my visit to Hell, the torment of it lasting for days, the heartbreak and trauma to my family, the lasting PTSD that affects all of us, and the horrendous, seemingly endless tug of war between good and evil, Heaven and Hell, life and death.

All of the other NDEs share this last part in common. Only the circumstances were different. The next one was in 2017. At the time, I was working two days a week due to my still-fresh cardiac condition. I was trying to stay active, see patients, and maintain an office in Beverly Hills.

We had lived in the San Bernardino Mountains since 2013 in our dream home—a beautiful oasis of majestic mountain beauty and isolation. Below is a picture from our backyard. Like all great things, it requires some sacrifice: in this case, the driving time to and from LA, UCLA, etc. That, and the winters, which are a big part of the adventure of living in the mountains. At times, they can be overwhelming and even dangerous, as pictures from the Blizzard of 2022 in subsequent chapters will show.

This is the view from the deck of our dream home in Lake Arrowhead, California, where summers are glorious and winters can be brutal.

The drive home from work was always about two-and-a-half to three hours, depending on traffic, and we'd usually arrive fairly late in the evening. There are no streetlamps on our street, but since I know it so well, I felt comfortable walking it even late at night without fear of the local wildlife. As far as I know, no one has ever been hurt or attacked by a bear.

There have been incidents where small dogs and cats have been carried away by coyotes, but nothing more than that. It's easy to say, unless it's your own dog or cat.

I had just returned from work with Claudia, and the first thing we had to do was walk our dog, Maximus, since the daytime dog sitter had already left. While Claudia was getting the house ready for bed, I let the dogs out and started walking them up the street to the cul-de-sac.

Even though it was pitch black, the stars illuminated the street and trees enough for me to feel comfortable walking to the end to let Maximus do his business. Like most people, I picked up my iPhone as soon as I parked the car in the garage and started catching up on emails and messages while walking.

As I walked toward the cul-de-sac, Maximus (a rare 120-pound male German Shepherd) was happily running around, growling and barking at nothing, as he often did.

Then, suddenly, everything went quiet.

The acoustics of our surroundings are such that you can almost hear a leaf drop, unless there's wind or a storm. We live in the woods, far from most of our neighbors, who aren't full-time residents. We can't sleep with the windows open because the birds' morning sounds drive us crazy. So, the sudden silence was unusual—there's usually something to bark at, like squirrels or foxes.

Distracted by my phone, I didn't notice the silence, which should have been deafening. Then I heard a bear growling, and Maximus came running out of the woods, making it hard to tell from which direction. Using my phone light, I saw two bear cubs coming from the woods ahead of me, followed by a much heavier crashing sound.

Had I been more cautious, I could have activated our streetlights from my phone, giving me a better idea of what was happening. It was clear that Maximus had stumbled upon a mama bear and her cubs—the most dangerous situation up here.

None of the "bear survival slogans" went through my mind. Instead, I turned and ran like a scared little girl down the street toward home. What I hadn't anticipated was Max running beside me, then suddenly cutting to the right as I ran downhill. His lunge caught me at the hip, and I was catapulted into an aerial barrel roll, crashing violently onto my left hip and fracturing it instantly.

The pain was excruciating—far worse than a heart attack or the pain from a car accident. I had lost my phone when I fell, and I was screaming for help. Maximus just sat still, staring at the bear and her cubs, and fortunately, they lost interest and walked away. This is what usually happens when a huge, snarling German Shepherd confronts them.

Max had encountered bears before, but that's another story. I could see my phone ringing as Claudia tried to call me, but I couldn't move without searing pain. I gave up on trying to reach it.

Claudia came outside, calling for me, likely thinking I was up the street, lost in thought. Given my cardiac history, I feared she might think something had happened to my heart. She had already been through so much, and I was more concerned about what this would do to her than what was happening to me.

I yelled that I wasn't okay, but it wasn't my heart! Maximus ran to her, then back to me, barking frantically. She ran to me, crying, and I tried to reassure her that I was stable—it was just a hip fracture. She pulled herself together, called 911, and our neighbor Bob came out to comfort me while we waited.

We live in a remote area, but I was surprised it took almost twenty minutes for 911 to arrive. I told them what happened, but they had to do their own assessment, delaying treatment further. When they tried to move me onto the gurney, the pain was so overwhelming I involuntarily fought them.

I hated that I couldn't control my screams, and Claudia had to hear all of it. Once again, we were in a crisis.

They loaded me into the ambulance, and Claudia followed me to the hospital. In the ER, I briefed them on my medical history, and the X-rays confirmed a left hip fracture.

I was admitted in the middle of the night, with an extensive cardiac history, on blood thinners, and an implanted defibrillator ready to fire. I was worried that jagged bone fragments could pierce arteries, so I suggested they check my blood counts every six hours. They seemed puzzled, but I knew this level of care was necessary.

The pain was unbearable, and I was kept in a Dilaudid fog to manage it. Still, I asked daily when my hip would be repaired. The answers were vague—there were OR availability issues, and the orthopedic surgeon was unavailable. I felt like I was in Canada, where waiting months for surgery is common. But I had Medicare and Blue Cross, so the delay made no sense. Hip fractures should be repaired within twenty-four hours.

Two days later, the hip was surgically repaired, but that delay was below the standard of care. I required blood transfusions due to blood loss before and during surgery.

I started to deteriorate and was transferred to the ICU with dropping blood pressure and low blood counts. The worst part was that, despite Claudia specifically telling them not to administer dopamine, they did. They were trying to stabilize me, but they didn't listen to Claudia.

Within seconds, I lost consciousness and went into ventricular tachycardia again. A code blue was called, and once again, my defibrillator fired, restoring my heart to a normal rhythm. I regained consciousness to Claudia's anguished face, and all I could do was apologize for putting her through this again.

This was my second pulseless ventricular arrhythmia and near-death experience.

Claudia described it as distinctive—she saw my face melt into a literal "death mask."[8] If you've ever seen one, it's unforgettable and haunting, the face losing all muscle tone. It's not something you'd associate with a living person. I've included a photo of a classic death mask on the next page.

---

[8] Death Mask of Italian Renaissance Architect Filippo Brunelleschi (1446) Made by His Adoptive Son Andrea di Lazzaro Cavalcanti, Called Buggiano, on Display in the Museo dell'Opera del Duomo, Museum of the Works of the Florence Cathedral in Florence, Tuscany, Italy," *Alamy,* accessed May 4, 2025, https://www.alamy.com/death-mask-of-italian-renaissance-architect-filippo-brunelleschi-1446-made-by-his-adoptive-son-andrea-di-lazzaro-cavalcanti-called-buggiano-on-display-in-the-museo-dellopera-del-duomo-museum-of-the-works-of-the-florence-cathedral-in-florence-tuscany-italy-image212520827.html.

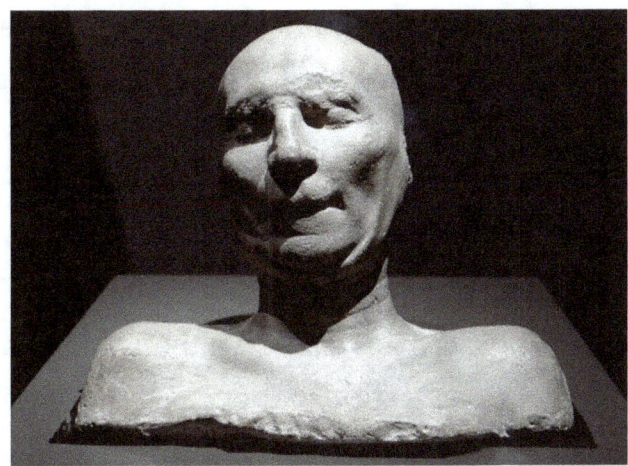

Claudia *said that when my face lost all muscle tone, I resembled the "Death Mask" of Italian Renaissance architect Filippo Brunelleschi (1446).[8] His adoptive son Andrea di Lazzaro Cavalcanti created this piece of art, which is called "Buggiano" and is displayed in the Museo dell'Opera del Duomo (Museum of the Works of the Florence Cathedral) in Florence, Italy. Claudia said this unforgettable and haunting image is seared in her mind.*

Everyone saw it. Before the crash cart could be in place, my implanted defibrillator fired and restored my heart to a normal rhythm.

They tried to remove Claudia from the room, and this time, they succeeded. She was physically drained, and the toll it was taking on her was evident. She didn't fight them—at least not for long.

I spoke with the critical care specialist and explained why we had been advised to avoid certain heart medications, as they had historically triggered potentially lethal arrhythmias.

Meanwhile, they started administering packed red blood cells (PRBCs) due to the significant blood loss before and during surgery. It felt like they only then realized the extent of the blood loss, starting lab tests and blood counts every six hours, as I had suggested upon admission.

I survived due to the defibrillator and the eventual response to my blood loss. However, each transfusion carries its own risks.

I can only describe the interval between consciousness and this near-death experience as the eerie "Hello, darkness, my old friend" feeling as expressed by the Paul Simon song, "The Sound of Silence." It's not funny or musical, but terrifying.

It made me realize that I hadn't been the same since the first NDE. These experiences leave a permanent mark.

This NDE lasted just long enough to send me into cold darkness, the sinking feeling returning with the anticipation of being sucked into that "cave of horrors" from the first time.

My main concern was Claudia. I was terrified because I knew another episode and shock were likely until they addressed my metabolic and hemodynamic issues.

Fortunately, no further episodes occurred during that hospitalization. After discharge, I focused on pain management, mobility, and rehabilitation from the hip replacement.

Within weeks, I was walking fairly normally again, and our focus shifted to the UCLA Cardiac Reversal

Protocols—keeping my heart functioning.

The third NDE occurred in 2019, about a year after the second. Over the course of these years, I'd had one episode annually since the heart attack in 2015, leading to the transplant in 2024.

The third NDE happened under the worst circumstances: I was driving with Claudia and my mother. We had just left The Grove shopping, dining, and movie complex in Los Angeles after seeing the film, *Ad Astra*. I was driving north on Fairfax toward Santa Monica Boulevard, one of the busiest intersections.

Claudia noticed me becoming unresponsive and began shaking me and screaming, "Rob! Rob! Rob!" I don't remember how long I was unconscious, but it takes about forty seconds for the defibrillator to charge and deliver a shock. Sometimes it takes multiple shocks.

Meanwhile, I was driving—unconscious!—at highway speed through an intersection. Miraculously, no one was hurt. I don't remember hitting the brake or putting the car in park, but Claudia managed to get me to stop at the crosswalk.

Confused and terrified, I was helped out of the driver's seat and into the back seat. Claudia rushed us to the hospital, where I was put on antiarrhythmic drugs. An angiogram revealed a new lesion, and they placed a third stent. Though I was discharged without further complications, the progression of my heart disease was undeniable. The dread of death lingered, and Claudia, who had witnessed these events, bore a heavy emotional toll.

The NDE was different this time because the chaos around me may have helped bring me back quicker. Still, it felt like the inevitable fear of death was never far away.

The fourth NDE occurred in 2020 while I was on the couch with Claudia and my mother. Claudia was shaking me and crying.

"Come back!" she pleaded.

I floated back into my body through the darkness, almost immediately regaining consciousness. I tried to reassure Claudia that I was okay, though I had no way of knowing if that was true. After each shock, I'd cling to the hope that things would stabilize—until the next one.

The randomness of these episodes made everything uncertain. We quickly drove to the hospital, where they administered antiarrhythmic drugs, hoping to stabilize my heart. The challenge was that I was already on oral versions of these drugs, and increasing the dose would only provide temporary relief.

We explored an ablation procedure, where they used heat or cold to destroy the scar tissue causing the arrhythmias. I underwent two ablations: one in 2021 and another in 2022. These procedures were grueling, requiring hours of anesthesia and a slow recovery.

Though the shocks continued leading up to my transplant, it was unclear whether the ablations had helped or just delayed the inevitable.

The fifth NDE in 2021 occurred unexpectedly after returning from errands. I was sitting on the bed, feeling the early signs of another episode. Claudia was there, and once again, I started slipping into unconsciousness from V-tach/V-fib.

Sometimes before I pass out, I experience a few seconds of feeling like I'm about to lose consciousness. This is often accompanied by a rapid heart rate and a complete inability to breathe. The terrifying sensation that I've stopped breathing while still conscious but unable to inhale no matter what, is indescribable. It's the literal terror of death, and I've experienced it many times.

This is called the prodromal phase. Most times, there's not enough time to fully feel it; I just pass out. But this time, I definitely felt it. There was just enough time to say something to Claudia like, "I don't feel right!" or "Help!"

Interestingly, most illnesses have a prodromal phase. In schizophrenia, it's marked by subtle changes in behavior—social withdrawal, unusual thoughts, and a decreased interest in activities—which can be mistaken for depression or anxiety. In infectious diseases, it usually includes general symptoms like fever, fatigue, and headaches before specific symptoms develop.

During my fifth NDE, my heart rate rapidly became irregular, causing my blood pressure to drop and my breathing to stop, which led to me collapsing backward onto the bed. Thankfully, I was sitting on it when it happened.

My defibrillator was able to perform something called overdrive pacing: pacing the heart faster than its natural rhythm to stop abnormal rhythms like V-tach or Supraventricular Tachycardia. It sends rapid electrical impulses to restore a normal rhythm. If that doesn't work, it sends a stronger defibrillation shock to correct the rhythm.

This was yet another nightmarish NDE, though there was no full loss of consciousness or shock this time. The event lasted only a couple of minutes—just long enough for me to experience that familiar drop away from life into the dark, cold cave of lost souls.

It included the delayed return to full consciousness and the horror of knowing I almost died again and almost had to endure another shock.

I had been sent home with a remote defibrillator inter-rogation device, which sent data directly to UCLA Health Cardiac Arrhythmia Center. Since I was within range of this device, it transmitted a recording of what happened. UCLA called to check on me, but no changes in therapy were recommended. I was instructed to continue the harsh combination of medications I was already on.

Claudia knew exactly what had happened. Although this event was somewhat less traumatic than the others, understanding the cause was unsettling and added another devastating notch to our belt of horrors.

It's worth considering that these devices don't always work. Batteries fail, electrodes loosen, and after multiple shocks, the heart might stop responding altogether.

Listing these events one after the other may sound clinical, but living through each one releases a torrent of emotion—sadness, euphoria, fear, apprehension, and relief all at once. After each event, another restless, sleepless night follows, filled with dreams about funerals and discussions with family.

Yet, every time, an even greater appreciation for life emerges, along with a heightened awareness of each precious moment we share together. After every event, Claudia and I would find ourselves in each other's arms, laughing and crying—mostly crying, praying that the transplant would put an end to this suffering.

Although we knew that a transplant would simply exchange one set of problems for another, there was no alternative. If you need a heart transplant, there's no other choice.

NDEs six and seven happened in 2022, while driving down Highway 18 with friends in the car. At least this time, I wasn't driving. I had stopped driving after my third NDE, when I nearly ran a red light on Fairfax and almost drove through an intersection full of people at Santa Monica Boulevard.

Interestingly, when I asked an electrophysiologist about driving, he told me I should keep driving. His reasoning was that there are far more people with undiagnosed arrhythmias who suddenly lose consciousness and die while on the road—at least with the defibrillator I had a chance! Perhaps a Tesla would help, but I couldn't live with that thought—especially not with friends or family in the car.

We had good friends visiting for the weekend, and Claudia was driving us down the hill for a day of shopping before taking them to the airport. If you're unfamiliar with Highway 18, it's a serious mountain road. We were used to it after more than a decade, but many aren't.

I remember we were having a good time talking when suddenly, I was deep in a fog of confusion, no longer moving in the right direction toward alertness and consciousness.

I knew I was in the car, and then the doors opened. We had stopped, and Claudia and the others were shaking me and yelling at me to "Wake up!" and "Come back!"

But instead of waking up, I felt myself sinking deeper into darkness, fading away. At that point, I was too far gone to be afraid, despite knowing I was dying—and this time, not coming back.

Then it hit me: the first semi-conscious full defibrillator shock. It felt like being kicked in the chest by a horse or shot by a shotgun—from within. It didn't seem real, and I still cringe at the thought. But when I consider the alternative—without that shock, the next thing would be death—I'm grateful for the implanted defibrillator that has saved me time and time again.

Later, I learned that I was shocked several times—once while fully unconscious and again while semi-conscious. The first shocks briefly restored my heart rhythm, but I fell back into V-tach/V-fib, requiring further shocks. This marked NDEs six and seven.

It's worth noting that the more shocks required to restore and maintain normal heart rhythm, the less my heart was responding to the defibrillator, which meant things were getting worse.

Our friends were deeply traumatized by what they witnessed. Though we'd explained the events to family and close friends, seeing it firsthand, as Amber did, made them fully realize how devastating it was—especially the aftermath. We dropped our friends off and then headed to the hospital. Sadly, that was the end of their weekend with us. They still talk about how it affected their lives and their awareness of mortality.

Some friends became more involved in our lives, calling more, visiting more. Others distanced themselves, as though being around us reminded them of something they didn't want to face. I don't blame them at all.

Honestly, I don't want visitors in the hospital, except for Claudia or close family. Hospital staff are rushed, often jumping into questions about immediate care that you may not want to share with visitors, who might gossip about it later. In transplant cases, it's even more serious, as the patient is immunocompromised to protect the transplanted organ. Anyone with a cold or worse poses a risk.

I had situations where people insisted on visiting, despite being told not to. Imagine the awkwardness of having to kick someone out because they don't understand the risks they're exposing you to, even with the best intentions.

On January 2, 2024, I experienced NDE and shock eight; on January 3, I survived NDE and shock nine—in Florida.

Claudia and I had flown to Florida to spend Christmas and New Year's with our children and grandchildren. We had a wonderful time, especially with our young grandchildren. I also had the chance to reconnect with old friends and enjoy New Year's with a dear psychiatrist friend while babysitting our grandchildren.

Then, on January 2, everything changed. I was getting dressed after a shower, reached for a drawer, and the next thing I knew, Claudia and Amber were shaking

214

me, trying to revive me after another cardiac arrhythmia event. 911 was already called, and it wasn't long before I was in the local hospital.

This was the hospital where I had worked for years, and the cardiologist in charge was someone I knew well. Clearly, our holiday trip had become a health emergency.

On January 3, I lost consciousness again, experienced another run of V-tach/V-fib, and was shocked again. This marked NDE nine. I was sitting up in bed, with Claudia present. A full code was called, but my defibrillator fired before anyone could respond, bringing me back to life.

The next week, tests revealed severe, recent cardiac deterioration, and angiograms showed rapid coronary artery disease, leaving too many blockages to treat with stents and too sick for open-heart surgery.

The doctors warned me that I was at high risk for a ventricular tachycardia storm—a cascade of shocks that would continue until my defibrillator couldn't keep up, resulting in a slow, horrific, torturous death.

After two shocks, Claudia's shaking lasted for hours, and I was terrified for her. After almost ten years of this, we couldn't handle much more.

The staff was exhausted and had little compassion. One code team member was annoyed to find me conscious and with a pulse. It was absurd, but I found it strangely funny.

The hospital suggested cutting the nerves to my heart to stop the fight-or-flight response, but things were rapidly falling apart. My heart was failing, and the blockages in my arteries were worsening. A transplant was my only hope, but I may have only had weeks or months to live.

That's when the situation took a bizarre turn: the hospital said I was too sick to be discharged, yet they could do nothing more for me. I was stuck in a place that had once been my workplace, with no answers.

In desperation, Claudia and our family tried to arrange for me to be airlifted to UCLA, but coordinating the air ambulance was a nightmare. Unable to make it work, Claudia made the executive decision to book a flight on JetBlue. It was leaving from Fort Lauderdale to Los Angeles at eight in the morning, so we signed out against medical advice at 5:00 a.m. during my second week in the hospital.

We knew that if anything happened on that flight, we were completely on our own, risking everything. If my defibrillator started firing, they would likely have had to make an emergency landing at the nearest airport—who knows where that could have been? Then, another ambulance, a hospital, and so on, unless I was strong enough to recover and catch another flight to LAX. It was a real nightmare. This wasn't idle speculation; it was highly probable.

Fortunately, it didn't happen.

After a harrowing flight, we arrived at LAX and went straight to the UCLA ER. thanks to the communication between Claudia and the transplant team prior to departure, I was admitted quickly.

The truth was, we "made it" to the beginning of another gauntlet: a completely new Open-Heart Transplant (OHT) workup, which would take about two weeks. I'd already gone through this process in 2017, qualifying for a heart transplant. But now, it was January 2024.

Since 2017, I've developed prostate cancer (treated with five intense radiation treatments) and a spinal tumor (meningioma), which had been removed in September 2023. The surgery left me with significant neurological damage, partial paralysis of my right arm, and other motor deficits in my right leg and neck.

Qualifying for and receiving a heart transplant was not a given anymore, though it was my final destination—either I'd qualify for a new heart, or I'd die from heart failure within weeks or months. Frighteningly, everyone agreed on that.

The next, and final, near-death experience (NDE)—number ten—was the heart transplant itself. Thankfully, I qualified and lived through it. Having your heart removed and spending hours on a heart-lung bypass machine qualifies as an NDE.

I was admitted to UCLA on January 9, 2024, and they wasted no time starting the open-heart transplant evaluation. Fortunately, the same decision-makers from 2017 were still in place and remembered Claudia and me.

Cardiac-wise, there was no question I needed a transplant, but the challenges lay in the prostate cancer and spinal tumor. The spinal tumor was histologically benign, but its behavior was malignant, causing spinal cord compression and nerve damage.

The tumor had made itself known in August 2023, causing my right leg muscles to fail and leading to a hip fracture. Unbelievably, I had a right total hip replacement in August and the spinal tumor removed in September—just months before I was admitted for the heart transplant.

The consensus was that the spinal tumor likely resulted from radiation exposure during my medical training. In those days, precautions were minimal, especially for interns and residents, who were exposed to high radiation levels while assisting in procedures.

Miraculously, my PSA was 0.3 (normal is 0-4.5), suggesting the prostate cancer was cured. The spinal tumor's recurrence risk was low, and it was very slow growing. I'd likely face heart transplant rejection issues before the tumor returned.

In the meantime, all other medical evaluations were

completed—everything from imaging and procedures to psychiatry for mental stability—and submitted to the Transplant Committee. This committee decides who is a suitable candidate for transplants, including hearts, lungs, and heart-lung combinations.

The first "box" they check is financial stability. Unfortunately, many people don't get a heart due to insurance or financial reasons. The second is a reliable family and caretaker support system. This means having two caretakers available 24/7 for at least three months and living within a certain distance of UCLA. Post-transplant, frequent lab tests and IV infusions are required, which profoundly disrupt normal life. Claudia, who does most of the driving, bears much of the burden.

I would not be allowed to fly for seven months after the transplant, and travel after that would depend on my recovery. Post-transplant, I would be on immunosuppressants, which would severely weaken my immune system to prevent rejection of the new heart. A simple cold could land me in the hospital for a week, so I would still need to isolate and avoid sick people as much as possible.

After completing the evaluation, I qualified for the transplant. The process took the usual two weeks, then the wait began. I was classified as Status IIIE (exception), meaning I couldn't leave the hospital until a compatible heart became available. This "exception" allowed me to stay in the hospital without a central line in my neck, as having any catheter inside my heart could trigger more dangerous arrhythmias.

Some people, like the ones we met during our stay, wait over a year for a heart. Tragically, some pass away before one becomes available. One friend received a heart but passed away weeks later due to complications. Thankfully, this was rare.

I was very fortunate that a compatible heart was located through the United Network for Organ Sharing (UNOS) within three weeks of being accepted as a candidate. My blood type and body size were crucial factors in this quick match.

Before the actual transplant, I had one false alarm. I was told a heart had been found and that I would be in the OR in hours. I panicked, thinking of the risks involved, especially the hours spent on a heart-lung bypass machine. I had seen many complications during my medical career, though none were linked to UCLA.

When the right heart was found, I was fortunate to have Dr. Abbas Ardehali, one of the top heart surgeons in the world. As a physician, I could see the respect he commanded, but he was kind and gracious to me and my family.

The heart came from Dallas, Texas, and was transported in a special "Sherpa Pack" to maintain temperature and fluid balance. We got the call on Valentine's Day, February 14th. Claudia had to watch me being wheeled away, terrified, not knowing if she'd ever see me alive again.

The next day, the transplant took about seven hours, with the OR team keeping Claudia updated via texts. The heart had reached the maximum allowed travel time—six hours—so Dr. Ardehali had to manually massage the heart for ninety minutes to get it to start pumping. The surgical team was concerned it might not work, and if it hadn't, that would have been the end for me.

This transplant process was more than just an NDE—it was beyond anything I could have imagined. If the heart had failed, I wonder where my soul would have ended up.

My son Bradley drove from Seattle and relocated for four months, arriving on the 16th to serve as the second full-time caretaker alongside Claudia. We rented an Airbnb to be closer to UCLA during this period.

I received the new heart on the 15th, was kept completely sedated in the ICU throughout the 16th, and was fully awakened and extubated—removed from the ventilator—on February 17th.

Claudia was there when I woke up, and Bradley arrived just a few hours later. Claudia was also present on the 16th when they partially woke me to test my breathing ability but quickly sedated me again after assessing my respiratory function. Claudia tells me I tried to communicate through hand gestures that first day.

The process of extubation was one of the worst experiences of my life, mainly because of the chest incision pain exacerbated by the necessary coughing.

I remember the first time in 2015 after I coded following the first near-death experience; for some reason, I recall it being much easier. This extubation after the transplant required a lot of coughing to clear my pulmonary secretions, and the pain from the chest incision was unbelievable, even with IV Dilaudid and other pain medications.

Claudia was there for the extubation, and I'm sure it was harder for her to watch than for me to endure. Once again, she had to witness nightmarish events happening to me. I hated that she had to go through this.

I was in the ICU for a little more than a week. It was a tough week, making me appreciate how easy I had it while waiting for the heart in the hospital. Of course, this time I had a new heart and just had to get through this immediate recovery period.

In the ICU, I was placed in a chair at 5:45 a.m. (the time didn't mean much since I was awake most of the time) and could order increasingly substantial food as the days progressed. The routine involved breakfast in the chair, followed by up to three extremely painful walks around the nursing stations (which became easier each day) spread throughout the day, along with physical and occupational therapy.

It amazed me how I was busy working to get stronger all day, every day, despite real pain from my chest incision, compounded by residual spinal pain issues from the spinal tumor removal.

I would walk with nurses, Claudia, and Bradley, who played the theme from the 1976 film "Rocky" to motivate me. I had chest tubes to inflate my collapsed lungs from surgery, which were removed after a couple of days, and a Foley catheter (a tube attached to me to collect urine, as I was too weak to use the commode for several days) was eventually taken out as well.

I looked a lot like Frankenstein, with all the scars, incisions, tubes, and wires attached to me, as I walked around with my son and wife holding me up and pushing me forward through the pain and muscular deconditioning I had to fight through.

I had a new twenty-five-year-old heart, but my sixty-seven-year-old body had weakened, severely deconditioned muscles and hadn't received proper, full blood circulation in ten years.

This new heart pounded so forcefully that it shook my body and caused the bed to rock as it beat. I could hear it beating when I tried to sleep, and it kept me up at night because it was so loud.

The obvious "elephant in the room" was and is constantly and palpably present: *Whose heart was this? How did he die? Who was he? Was he a good person or a murderer? In other words, was he good or evil?*

We were told the donor was male, about twenty-five, and similar in stature to me (he had to be for the heart to fit). We were also informed that he was from Dallas, Texas.

This is something I have to deal with every day. I think about it at night, and all the possible implications, nuances, conjectures, and wonders are what Claudia and I wrestle with all the time. We talked about it constantly, especially during this time in the ICU. We think about the donor family and their loss. We grieve for them and for the person who donated this, my heart.

We wrestle with whether to write the family a letter—something the transplant team addresses extensively, and we have received counseling on all these issues. There is much more that needs to be said about this, and I will address it later. For now, suffice it to say that I'm having trouble deciding whether I want to know who it was that "gave" me this heart or what he looked like or what his life was like.

Claudia is much more of a detective than I am and likely knows more about the donor and the donor family than I do. But I have asked her not to tell me for now because, frankly, I can't handle it yet. It wouldn't be too difficult to search the obituaries for young men who passed away on Valentine's Day 2024 in Dallas.

I cared for ICU patients for decades, with all kinds of the most serious diagnoses, but nothing prepared me for the ICU experience following a heart transplant—not as a doctor and certainly not as a patient.

The last two days in the ICU were the worst. One of the cardiologists on the transplant team wanted to perform a heart biopsy (literally going into my heart through veins in my neck to take three pieces of my heart wall to assess for signs of rejection).

I have had nine heart biopsies to date, and they never really got any easier.

I am grateful and honored for our loved ones and friends who visited with the best intentions. However, sometimes people feel compelled to visit sick friends or relatives to make themselves feel better. Forgive me for saying this, but it is the truth—something I learned and observed through this process.

This was undeniably true when we clearly said no to visitors, yet they came anyway, unable to comprehend the immunosuppression issues and need for isolation involved in this transplant process. Not to mention our being overwhelmed and basically "out of words." Exhausted. Done. Finished.

In a hospital, people come and go continuously, and patients simply tire of having to interact 24/7. Some visitors may be motivated by guilt over unresolved issues when realizing the person in the hospital is potentially facing death. Others may have wanted to visit to remain in Claudia's good graces, thinking that visiting me would have that effect. It didn't.

It's merely stating a fact that Claudia is an extremely attractive, fun, energetic, and popular person, always becoming a social nucleus wherever we spend time. I include these observations because they are interesting regarding how people behave in these situations. It's useful to remember that the patient's needs should be prioritized at times like this.

When one is completely vulnerable and broken down, it's important to reflect on how long-standing friends and even some family behaved. A friend once said it's when you're in prison or the hospital that you learn who the people in your life really are. I have never been in prison or even arrested (except for one time in Mexico . . . but that's a story for another day), but it's an interesting observation.

Let's return to the transplant and the difficult ongoing recovery. From transplant to hospital discharge took about two weeks. During the last week, in addition to strengthening efforts, medication adjustments, and aggressive invasive anti-rejection treatments (PT, OT, forced marches, etc.), a huge amount of time was dedicated to patient and caretaker education.

There were mandatory, all-hands-on-deck teaching sessions that lasted all day with virtually no warning. We were given large tomes on the transplant and post-transplant periods to read. I was told my "support group"—Claudia and Bradley—had to be present the entire day tomorrow at 9:00 a.m., and that was that. Bradley was working remotely with Microsoft but still had meetings and other commitments. Claudia was managing caring for my mother, our finances and bills, two homes (including the Airbnb), and the transplant process, so dropping everything with no notice was just one more stressor.

Of course, we did everything with sincere gratitude for the miracle of a new heart and a new life, but the difficulties of the process were what they were. Gratitude, joy, and prayerful humility were how we viewed this journey, coupled with sheer awe on my part at the skills of the attending physicians and transplant team. My graphic description of the process is to accurately and honestly convey what this has been like.

Eventually, the day came for my discharge from the hospital. I was discharged to Claudia and Bradley, and the drive to the rented Airbnb was filled with cheers, crying, and laughter that I had survived and was out of the hospital! Of course, this was just the beginning of the expected two or three times per week follow-up visits at UCLA, and we never missed a beat. The process is still ongoing, and we still don't miss a single appointment or anything they ask us to do.

I was profoundly exhausted, with home physical therapy, home nursing, and home occupational therapy every day, in addition to the back and forth from UCLA, I had good reason to be. I found myself falling asleep pretty much all the time, as soon as I could sit down anywhere. I would nap a lot during the days between therapies—all of which was normal.

I still had to endure sometimes weekly heart biopsies and other admissions and procedures, and the ongoing back and forth from the Airbnb to UCLA and back. We were finally given permission to return to our home in Lake Arrowhead in early June.

Everyone was deeply concerned about the altitude being a problem, as we live at 6,000 feet. I knew it wouldn't be an issue, as I had a twenty-five-year-old heart that was working well, and there was nothing wrong with my lungs. I watched my oxygen saturation closely, and it was never a problem. Most commercial airliners are pressurized to about 5,000 feet, so this wasn't much different. Supplemental oxygen or a pressurized cabin in an aircraft isn't really needed until you get over about 10,000 feet.

I'm writing this at the end of July, and it took until about now for my vitality (limited by the spinal cord injury issues from the spinal tumor) to start returning. Keeping in mind that I am attending cardiac rehabilitation—strenuous, intense, supervised exercise at UCLA twice a week. I still have to go to a transplant clinic twice a month, soon to be once a month, but our lives—compared to the recent past—are starting to return to some semblance of normalcy.

At this point, I can walk on the level parts of our street for an hour and a half at a time and going up and down three flights of stairs all day is not a problem. Thank you, Jesus. No more V-tach or V-fib—ever. No more defibrillators. No more shocks. No more near-death experiences!

Chapter 9

Miracles Brighten the Hell of Now

By Dr. Rob

While our new "now" is in no way Hell, what we've endured over the last ten years arguably qualifies as a kind of Hell. Yet Claudia and I held onto each other so tightly through every step, horror, and painful procedure that our appreciation for the blessing of each other and family has evolved into something resembling a sacrament (no disrespect or blasphemy intended).

It's hard to conceive of what we've been through and come out alive, so far, as anything short of an actual, real-life miracle (again, no blasphemy intended).

What does recovery look like at this point, five months into the new heart at the time of writing this?

The recovery process remains hard. It requires discipline and relentless commitment to an almost impossible medication schedule, as well as lab and transplant clinic schedules. There's also the knowledge that I might be called back into the hospital at any time because of an elevated donor-specific antibody count from last week's labs or anything else that's out of whack. It's very stressful constantly worrying about running out of medications or keeping track of the status and remaining amount of all these medications.

I take twenty-three pills in the morning, a slightly smaller number in the evening, and three or four mid-day. None of these medications make me feel "good." But this is necessary to prevent rejection and manage complications such as high blood pressure, possible fluid overload, and other issues that arise in the early phases after a transplant.

The most common cause for hospital admission after a heart transplant in the first three months is fluid overload, or congestive heart failure, because the body hasn't yet accommodated the changes in circulation. I weigh myself twice a day and take Lasix (a "water pill" or diuretic that causes me to urinate excessive fluid) if my weight goes up, my rings get tight, or my socks leave an imprint on my legs (edema).

And yet, we wake up every morning thanking God for another day together, with a quirky smile—like it's unreal to be waking up together at all. Because it is!

What does the future hold?

Hopefully, as signs of rejection become more sup-pressed and controlled, fewer visits to UCLA will be needed, granting us more freedom to travel and be around people. Ideally, we'll reach a point where only twice-a-year visits are required, and we'll be free to travel and do whatever else we want—always simply filled with joy at just being together and being alive.

Acutely aware of the joy and miracle of just being alive, always.

I remain prayerful, repentant, and humble—having been completely leveled, destroyed, and left utterly helpless and humiliated through this process. Repeatedly. In every way.

I vividly remember the "visitors" who came unexpectedly, only to have me lose control of my bowels all over the room, furniture, hospital gown, and everything else. My body had not yet become able to handle the side effects of the anti-rejection medications and gastrointestinal dysregulation was prominent among them. Much of it ended up on them because one of them totally freaked out and started walking around the room in circles, screaming, "OMG! OMG!" and spreading the mess everywhere. It's pretty funny now, but it was horrible and humiliating at the time.

Why has my attitude and outlook changed so radically? Because I don't want to go to Hell again. I know the arrogant, self-important doctor and "high-powered" persona I perceived myself to be—financially successful and on staff at five hospitals at a time, at one point—and

I know where that pride will get me, along with my horrendous past sins and failure to understand redemption through Christ.

I reached the pinnacle of medical practice: on executive committees, ethics committees, peer review committees; I was a partner in a lucrative air ambulance company, enjoying the benefits of patients' full-coverage international travel insurance coverage for medical bills, etc.

After reaching and knowing this "pinnacle," I was cast down to the bottom of the medical heap for a time. I was humbled all along the way and didn't recognize why. I have been sued for medical malpractice and lost; I have also been sued and won (e.g., wrongful death cases where I was medical director for a physician group and dragged into cases where I never saw or treated the patient).

I endured medical record audits that resulted in severe licensing repercussions and penalties—again, responsible for medical records of physicians in a group setting, as well as my own medical records, which had deficiencies.

I lost a $4.3 million case involving a Pap smear in June 2000 because Quest Labs misread a Pap smear slide as essentially normal when it was a wildly undifferentiated cancer, resulting in the tragic death of a twenty-two-year-old young woman.

I had to sit, completely alone, every day through the two-week trial at the Broward County Courthouse, facing the grieving family, attorneys, judge, and everyone else involved in this case, for which I felt so helpless and sad for the patient and her family. I was also afraid of reprisals or vengeance from the unfortunate family, and none of my family or friends were there for a single day to support me.

At least these cases are not on my list of reasons why I went to Hell, nor do they haunt me as do others I've described before. I don't mean this in a callous way at all—but I consider these cases to be the risk you take when practicing medicine and "the cost of doing business" in the current medico-legal environment. These things were out of my control, despite my best intentions and dedication to the highest patient care I could provide.

However, professionally, these cases were costly, destructive, and nearly ruinous at one point. Fortunately, I emerged with my California medical license intact, free, and clear.

God kicked my ass over and over again because it took losing me completely, in every sense of the word, to find Him.

What is the meaning behind all of this? I guess that's the question, isn't it? Who am I to answer it? All I can do is share the meaning Claudia and I got out of this, without pretense of having "the" answer or anything else.

One of the meanings is that I have been given the opportunity to write this and maybe that's the answer to the question: *What is the meaning behind all this?* The answer is understanding and actively living in the spirit of God and the power of love and faith.

Chapter 10

Learning to Live

By Dr. Rob

Now that I had mastered dying, it was time to learn how to live.

I realized how easy and effortless it is to die. Fighting to stay alive is the real challenge. You actually need to "learn to live" to get it right—or at least, less wrong.

While at UCLA, before being discharged from the hospital, Claudia, Bradley, and I attended patient education sessions that were all-day and mandatory. These one-on-one classes focused on what it truly means to "learn to live."

A lot of the material reflected the Cardiac Illness Reversal Program that we attended in 2017. (Remember—"there's one more thing you can do.") The program was started by Dr. Arnold Baas and later continued by others under his supervision.

We were ahead of the curve, having already gone through it in 2017, so most of it was a refresher—how to eat, and more importantly, how *not* to eat. Essentially, it was about following an ultra-low-fat, low-sodium, heart-healthy diet.

However, this time, it was more complicated. I had to avoid foods or supplements that could conflict with the anti-rejection medications that I was taking. I also had to steer clear of anything not fully cooked or pasteurized due to my weakened immune system. I had to wear a mask everywhere (and still do frequently in high-risk environments) and I had to avoid exposure to people to avoid contagion.

In other words, I had to continue to avoid the "modifiable" cardiac risk factors I could control, but now, I was literally on steroids and multiple other anti-rejection medications.

If you want to avoid ending up like me—on a heart transplant list, or worse—you may want to learn about and manage these risk factors. The earlier in life you start, the longer you'll live and the fewer preventable problems you'll face. Try to include and influence your family and children to do the same.

These risk factors that you can control include, but are not limited to:

- High blood pressure
- Unhealthy blood cholesterol levels
- Elevated blood sugar
- Diabetes mellitus
- Obesity
- Inadequate physical activity

- Lack of stress management
- Excessive alcohol consumption
- Smoking and being exposed to secondhand smoke

A lot of this may seem obvious, but sometimes the obvious needs to be stated. Less obvious, but worth mentioning, are cardiac risk factors that we cannot control or change. These include:

- Age
- Gender
- Race
- Family history of heart disease
- Genetic predispositions that cause blood clots or other heart issues

As doctors, we've seen it all: the patient who never smoked but developed lung cancer; the super-fit athlete who drops dead from a sudden arrhythmia; or the young athlete who collapses from a condition like Wolff-Parkinson-White syndrome, which is a reentry arrhythmia that can be treated if diagnosed in time. I also treated a patient hospitalized six times for endocarditis, an infection of the heart valves caused by sharing infected needles while using heroin. She needed six weeks of IV antibiotics but continued her destructive addiction.

We've also encountered patients we call "immortals"—people who survive seemingly impossible odds.

One memorable example was "Broken Brenda," a woman who jumped from a six-story building in a suicide attempt. Despite breaking most of the bones in her body, she survived years of hospital stays, complications, and surgeries. She even managed to fall out of bed and break her hip, eventually transferring to orthopedic care. It sounds bizarre, but ask any experienced physician, and they'll verify similar stories.

The point is, staying healthy isn't always under anyone's control. Genetic predispositions, like those that contribute to cancer, or genetic errors affecting heart development, can lead to children needing heart transplants.

It's a good idea for you to get annual check-ups that include blood work so that you are aware of your numbers that indicate your wellness, and where you might need to make lifestyle changes to improve them. Here's an overview, based on guidelines from the American Heart Association.

Blood Pressure Categories

- **Normal:** Less than 120/80 mm Hg
- **Elevated:** 120–129/<80 mm Hg
  (May be improved through lifestyle changes)
- **Hypertension, Stage 1:** 130–139/80–89 mm Hg
  (May require lifestyle changes and possibly medication)
- **Hypertension, Stage 2:** 140+/90+ mm Hg

(Often requires lifestyle changes and two-drug therapy)

Lipid Management (Cholesterol)

- **LDL (Low-Density Lipoprotein):** Under 100 mg/dL = *Optimal*
- **Total Cholesterol:** Under 200 mg/dL = *Desirable*
- **HDL (High-Density Lipoprotein):** Over 60 mg/dL = *Protective*
- **Triglycerides:** Under 150 mg/dL = *Normal*

Obesity Criteria

- **Body Mass Index (BMI):** Greater than 30 = *Obese*
- **Waist Circumference:**
- Men: Greater than 102 cm / 40 inches
- Women: Greater than 88 cm / 35 inches

 (Elevated risk for cardiovascular disease and metabolic disorders)

Fasting Glucose Levels

- ***Normal:*** Less than 100 mg/dL
- ***Prediabetes:*** 100–125 mg/dL (increased risk for diabetes)
- ***Diabetes:*** 126 mg/dL or higher on two separate tests

Note: A fasting glucose of 100 mg/dL or higher is considered a risk factor for type 2 diabetes and cardiovascular disease.

Sedentary Lifestyle

A sedentary lifestyle is defined as engaging in less than 150 minutes per week of moderate-intensity physical activity (for example, brisk walking), or exercising fewer than three times per week.

Health Risk: A sedentary lifestyle is associated with increased risk for cardiovascular disease, obesity, type 2 diabetes, and more.

You can find these recommendations from many sources. For the purposes of this writing, these recommendations come from the "ITNS Heart Transplant Handbook: A Guide For Your Health Care after Heart Transplantation" that UCLA physicians provided for me.[9]

It's truly amazing how many diseases can be avoided or modified in a positive way by simply maintaining a healthy weight and being physically active every day. Taking action to manage stress and depression is extremely beneficial as well; exercise is literally an antidepressant because it releases feel-good hormones that boost mood, improve sleep, and increase energy.

Every person's destiny and lifespan are shaped by complex, interrelated factors. At the end of the day, all we can really do is pray, ask for the blessing of longevity, and do our best to stay healthy by using the knowledge above.

---

[9] Sandy Cupples et al., *A Guide to Your Health Care After Heart Transplantation*, International Transplant Nurses Society, supported by an educational grant from XDx, 2011, accessed May 4, 2025.

As Claudia revealed in Chapter 2, she suffered from "Broken Heart Syndrome"—a temporary heart condition that is triggered by intense physical and/or emotional stress. It's a graphic, terrifying example of how extreme, ongoing stress can damage the heart. Claudia developed arrhythmias similar to mine; they were so serious that they required an ablation and implantation of a heart-monitoring device.

It may seem unfair that Claudia had to endure this alongside other significant health problems, but it is yet another way she had to learn to live. This is also an example of how love and life are inseparable. Many spouses, for instance, pass away shortly after their loved ones do, so deep is their bond.

Claudia also struggled to be heard as a woman, advocating for proper care in the face of substandard treatment. Despite her substantial medical knowledge and experience managing clinics, she was often dismissed or belittled by those who should have been more understanding.

Ironically, the source of her battles were often highly educated, well-trained professionals—the very ones you'd expect to respect her. Through it all, she learned to fight for me and advocate for my life.

We both learned that confrontational skills are necessary tools for survival. Advocating for oneself is part of learning to live.

Chapter 11

Unsung Heroes—Claudia, Bradley, My Mother, Our Family, and Some Not-So-Heroic Others

By Dr. Rob

The staggering personal sacrifice, selfless dedication, and commitment required from family during the pre- and post-transplant process are beyond description until you live through it. The costs—health consequences, the moving and rental costs of an Airbnb to be close to UCLA, separation from loved ones (due to prolonged isolation to avoid contagion), and the relocation required for three to six months—are overwhelming.

Caretaker situations are known to be among the unhealthiest and stress-inducing. Claudia gave, and continues to give, one hundred percent of herself in every imaginable way. This "situation" has lasted for ten years. She has had to witness the unimaginable.

Claudia has canceled countless trips to see her daughters, Ashley and Amber, in Florida, along with our grandchildren and their birthdays. For a decade, she has watched me suffer and literally die over and over again, all at once. Imagine how regretful and sad this makes us both feel. Thankfully, we've been blessed with more time—hopefully decades—and can now look forward to making up for lost moments. Our children and grandchildren love and support us in every way and understand what's at stake, so hopefully with time we can make up for those lost hallmark moments.

All the while, the cost to Claudia's health has been near-fatal. She has endured more than two years of worsening gastric pain that developed into ulcers, which are now under control with medication. In the last two years, she developed diverticulitis, requiring multiple painful hospitalizations. Ultimately, she underwent surgery at UCLA on July 2, 2024, to remove twenty-eight inches of her intestines. She is still recovering.

If that weren't enough, Claudia developed a heart conduction system disorder, leading to episodes of Supraventricular Tachycardia (SVT). This dangerous, rapid arrhythmia required an invasive and frightening ablation to stop its origin.

Though largely managed with the procedure and medication (beta-blockers), the problem persists.

Claudia has an implanted loop heart monitor in her right breast, which is constantly transmitting data to her cardiologist. Breakthrough episodes still occur, scaring us both. Fortunately, they are now transient. However, cardiologists believe her condition is progressive and, eventually, she will need an implanted defibrillator to protect her from worsening arrhythmias, which is typical of this condition.

This severe and ghastly development is known as "Broken Heart Syndrome." Watching me suffer has literally broken her heart's electrical conduction system. By the grace of God, she didn't have a heart attack, and an angiogram showed clear, wide-open coronary arteries. This confirms that the issue is stress related.

All of this is a direct consequence of what we've been through.

Bradley, while not facing any health issues, had to leave his life in Seattle, relocating to Los Angeles to be close to UCLA. We stayed in the Airbnb for about four months. This was just the latest instance where he dropped everything to help us. Whether he was in Seattle or Florida, he never hesitated to come when we needed him.

Living in the San Bernardino Mountains is beautiful but presents unique challenges. The winters, with heavy snow, and our two large dogs—Maximus and Sparticus (a seventy-pound mix of German Shepherd, Malinois, Jindo, and Rottweiler)—make it difficult to travel. These dogs, along with our calico cat, Kicia, cannot be left alone overnight. Family or trusted friends must take turns caring for them, especially when one of us is hospitalized. When things get tough, it's simply too much for just the two of us to manage alone.

Not everyone can handle the dogs or the snow and wild weather, but Claudia and Bradley are among the few who can. They can navigate these challenges and help prevent damage to our home so everything functions no matter what.

Following are pictures from the Blizzard of 2022. We were stranded for a dangerous amount of time, given our health conditions. This once-in-a-lifetime blizzard caused homes and businesses to collapse under the weight of the snow, rupturing gas lines, starting fires, and tragically, even claiming lives ninety miles east of Los Angeles.

The snow was so high that it reached the second floor of our home. We were trapped in the house for two weeks. This was before the transplant. No 911 service was available, and we were terrified of another cardiac event. The blizzard inspired neighbors to come together to help each other in a way I'd never experienced.

Bradley's Detours on my Healing Journey

Despite being able to work remotely, Bradley still missed numerous important meetings and faced other work-related stressors. As I've said, he and Claudia relocated to an Airbnb near UCLA immediately after my hospital discharge from UCLA after the heart transplant. On top of numerous scheduled trips to UCLA, they had to carry me upstairs, help me change clothes, and assist me in going to the bathroom during the early stages of my recovery. This was a tremendous strain on both of them.

Bradley, a dedicated outdoorsman, would normally spend his weekends hiking, fishing, or snowboarding. Instead, he and Claudia assisted me every day as I grew stronger over the months. He lost time with friends and his significant other, and Claudia lost time with everyone—her friends and family. This continues for Claudia due to my suppressed immune system, which is necessary to prevent rejection of my new heart. And it imposed restrictions on when I could fly in an airplane.

My mother, with whom I am extremely close, lives in an assisted living facility. As a result, I can't visit her, have dinner with her, or even ride in a car with her due to her exposure to pathogens from the communal living situation. As I write, she is recovering from COVID-19, which is almost endemic in these environments. Thank

God for FaceTime, which allows us to see our family and loved ones when we can't be together in person.

Happy Birthday, Mom. Claudia and I celebrated my mother Beatrix's birthday on February 17, 2018, at The Smokehouse restaurant.

These are just some of the burdens my family has endured during this ongoing process. I am humbled by their sacrifices and love for me. To see how highly my life is valued is both an honor and a blessing, though I don't feel worthy of it.

In contrast, I have also seen an excruciating example where a wife abandoned her sick husband because taking care of him was too much. This happened not because she was physically incapable, but because it was too much trouble. She said it wasn't fair for her life to be ruined by caring for him. Some of her friends even encouraged her to leave. Her wheelchair-bound husband was fed TV dinners (since she wouldn't cook) and needed help with almost everything. His family, though nearby, had limited availability and commitment. He wasn't placed in extended care, nor was there any attempt to explore that option.

Like a grim fairy tale, the wife secretly packed her things and abruptly told him she was leaving for a couple of days to visit family. Despite his pleas, she flew across the country. In love, hardships shouldn't drive people apart. The moral of this story is to be cautious about who you choose to weather life's storms with.

Claudia and I have been through the fire—numerous "in sickness and in health" moments—and we've held onto each other even harder, loving each other more passionately as we face these health challenges. We've both gone through the gauntlet, along with our families, who have risen to the challenge and been there when we needed them most. Bradley and Amber, with a newborn and her husband Alan, have come to our side before and after surgeries and procedures.

I share this because it's vital to understand that you can't take for granted that your spouse, significant other, family, or friends will always be there for you in the ways you need them. It's not just about token visits to make people feel better about themselves.

Another critical lesson is to make your own plans and provisions for your later years. If you don't, it may be too late when you need them, and others will make decisions for you—likely choosing the least desirable or most uncomfortable option. Do you really want to be a burden to your children and limit their ability to enjoy their own lives?

Individual financial and cultural factors play a role, but these are general observations made acute by my years in medical practice and our own experiences over the past eleven years. Sadly, most of the people I've seen die in hospitals passed away alone. In some hospitals, groups of nurses stay after their shifts in street clothes to sit with dying patients who have no one else. They hold hands, talk to them, and pray with them as they pass. It's incredible, beautiful, and inspiring to witness such love and compassion.

Choose your spouses and friends carefully, and cultivate authentic, loving, committed relationships. Ask yourself now: *Will the people around me stand by me until the end? Am I trusting the right people with sensitive financial and personal information?*

When you marry, you marry your spouse *and* their family. Take a good look at their family. Avoid toxic, petty, and negative people who are emotional vampires. They can suck the joy, fun, love, and even your health out of your life.

There are many proverbs about "children of darkness" who are restless unless plotting evil, as described in Isaiah 57:20: "The wicked have no rest; they are like the troubled sea, which cannot be still, whose waters cast up mire and dirt."

It's well known in psychiatry that one in ten people suffers from serious mental illness. If these individuals infiltrate your inner circle, they can do real damage. I'm not referring to family members who suffer from mental illness and need love and support; I'm referring to those driven by resentment, jealousy, ignorance, or evil who would harm you if allowed. Beware of wolves in sheep's clothing.

Consider this, according to the National and Unidentified Persons System (NamUS), more than 600,000 people go missing in the U.S. each year, with about 4,400 unidentified bodies recovered annually. Though this is not the place to speculate, it's something to consider when thinking about how to stay alive and protect yourself.[10]

Lastly, most people will betray you, not out of malice, but because of weakness. For instance, the coworker

---

[10] National Institute of Justice, "About," *National Missing and Unidentified Persons System (NamUs)*, accessed May 4, 2025, https://namus.nij.ojp.gov/about.

who makes you look bad in front of your boss, the neighbor who reports you to the homeowner's association for minor violations, or people who ask for loans or investments when you and your spouse are distracted. These individuals are taking advantage of "crimes of opportunity," revealing their lack of character.

I thank God every day for the unsung heroes in my life—Claudia, Bradley, my mom, our daughters, Amber, Ashley, Alan, and all our extended family. I can't imagine what I did right to deserve them, especially Claudia, who took a huge leap of faith when she married me.

Thank you, Jesus, God the Father, and the Holy Spirit for my unsung heroes. Please protect us from those who wish us harm and open the eyes and ears of those who are lost, so they too may find their own unsung heroes.

Chapter 12

On Spirituality

By Dr. Rob

Talking about spirituality is both easy and difficult after all we've been through together. Remember the "meat grinder" analogy? Well, we are now the sausage that came out.

I know what I'm about to say will make me a target. People will scoff, insult me, or suggest I lack sophistication, and in general, attack me for my beliefs. That's great! It means I'm doing something right. I'm writing this out of love, to share a gift with you.

I know what I know, and I've lived through things that have shown me this gift. In Matthew 7:6, Jesus says, "Do not give what is holy to the dogs; nor cast your pearls before swine, lest they trample them under their feet, and turn and tear you to pieces." This means not offering something valuable to those who won't appreciate it. Be discerning when sharing wisdom, kindness, or valuable resources.

Going through the complete destruction of life forces you into the spiritual realm. Ultimately, that's a good thing, but going to Hell or almost losing a beloved soulmate and her health is obviously not ideal. Maybe that's why Buddhist monks and others in search of spiritual connection practice self-deprivation and deep meditation, using bells and repeating "Ohm" to find entry points.

The spiritual connection between Claudia and me is real and palpable. We know we'll never lose each other because we are connected in Christ, all day, every day. As Matthew 18:20 says, "For where two or three gather in my name, there I am with them." God's presence is with those who gather in His name, regardless of the number.

The obvious entry point for spiritual connection is to pray, read the Bible, and enter the "zone" with intense concentration. When I first read the Bible, I did it at night, reading to my young sons as they fell asleep. I later read it to myself—cover to cover, several books multiple times. I still refer to it daily, which helps me remain "in the Spirit" and aware of my surroundings.

Reading it, I realized that its timeless wisdom and knowledge were beyond any human to write. There was a higher power embedded in the text, impossible to miss. That power becomes yours through faith.

It wasn't until Claudia and I experienced near-death experiences (NDEs) and everything that came with it—especially my "aha" moment when I understood why I went to Hell—that everything became clearer. My life was judged and found wanting.

That was when I truly understood what it means to have a personal relationship with Jesus. He suffered and died on the cross so that I wouldn't have to. I have repented, and I am redeemed. Ultimately, it's about redemption and freedom from anxiety about death, separation from Claudia, my family, and what comes after.

This does not mean I exclude or look down on people with different beliefs. In John 10:16, Jesus says, "I have sheep that are not of this fold. I must bring them also." He is the shepherd to many flocks. I don't need to worry about others' paths—He has it covered.

Technically, I am a Roman Catholic. But I'm no longer constrained by the legalistic rules of the Catholic Church or any other denomination. If you actually read the Bible, you'll find passages that contradict the teachings of the Catholic Church. For instance, Matthew 23:9 says, "And call no man your father on earth, for you have one Father who is in Heaven." This encourages believers to recognize God's unique role, not elevate earthly figures like priests to divine status.

This doesn't exclude biological fathers; it's about understanding the deeper spiritual message.

Experiencing death and resuscitation and feeling the power of God's love through Claudia's strength, clarified everything for me. The transformational power of faith and God changes everything for you and your soulmate as you go through life's worst storms.

Her desperate prayers, which brought me back to life, made me realize the simplicity of spirituality: live fully awake, aware of every moment, and live in the "NOW" with spiritual situational awareness. A soulmate, and ideally family, anchored in the Spirit, makes everything easier.

But what if you're alone with no soulmate? That's much harder. You first need to learn to love and value yourself. Ask yourself why you are alone. But that's a different story about learning to truly love yourself and God, free from the negative distractions that would destroy your spirit.

In that situation, double down on reading the Bible and surrounding yourself with people of faith. The God within you will be palpable to those around you, and you will find happiness and freedom, likely no longer alone, and perhaps even on the road to finding your own soulmate—God willing.

Finding God and someone to love with the same mindset is the ultimate goal and key to peace and happiness. Life isn't always peaceful, but it's how we handle these challenges that matters.

There is a realm of angels, demons, and rivers of the damned and saved. Hell is real, and you want no part of it—believe me.

Learn to be still, silent, receptive, and open-minded as you work and pray to connect with God the Father, the Son, Jesus, and the Holy Spirit. It's a tough ask, but if you can learn to be still and silent, trusting that He is God and committing everything to Him, He will fight your battles for you. You can relax and enjoy life and be happy. It really is that simple. It's part of the key to the success of Claudia and my happiness in the face of ongoing life challenges.

Chapter 13

Love Relationships

By Dr. Rob

I knew the moment I saw Claudia that I was going to love her—and that she would love me back. I loved her instantly, and although she didn't fully realize it yet, her smile told me she knew too.

Our love never wavered and only grew stronger with each mind-blowing challenge and hardship. However, the course of our lives did not run smoothly, and we could never have imagined just how bumpy the journey would be. What an adventure!

Initially, for various reasons, everyone in both our worlds opposed our union. Without delving into details, I can't entirely blame them, looking back eleven years later. I was a very different person then, and Claudia's love has virtually remade me into a much better man. That's why I admire her so much—for her courage and the huge leap of faith she took in trusting me, relocating across the country, and marrying me.

I'd like to believe that everyone who opposed our union has thoroughly changed their minds by now. Claudia was always the social nucleus of her world in Florida, and none of her friends wanted to see her leave them to move to California with me—a man they neither knew nor liked at the time. She has always been deeply loved by her friends, and she loves them back.

That's not to say either of us loved anyone in our worlds any less. For the first time, however, we had found real, once-in-a-lifetime, romantic, and reality-based, soul-locked, and soul-mated love. Both of us had endured previous disastrous marriages and all the painful consequences that came with them, so we were confident we knew what we were doing this time.

This brings me to the topic of advocating for yourself against all odds, even when those odds include the people you've known the longest. Taking a chance on love requires tremendous courage, self-confidence, and a sincere thirst for a happy life—perhaps for the first time. It's easy to get comfortable with your life situation, and it's even easier for your friends to get comfortable with it. No one likes change. It threatens everyone's sense of stability and normalcy. Sometimes, you realize that no matter what you do in your life, it's never good enough for others. You have to learn to shut out the noise and focus on living true to yourselves—and just do your best for everyone else.

Ultimately, change doesn't happen on your time or according to your plans. Change happens on God's time—while He laughs at your plans. And just like forcing your way through a difficult divorce, sometimes you have to step out of your comfort zone and take a long shot at great cost to forge a happy and free life for yourselves.

To avoid being inappropriate or embarrassing our children, I'll just say that the chemistry between us was—and still is—like an eternal flame that only burns more brightly as time passes. Our adult children were set on their own trajectories. Our daughters had their own lives, and my sons were leaving for college (UF) within weeks. It was now or never for Claudia and me to move to California. Thank God, against all odds, we made that "now" work.

We got to experience the "power of now," the joy of having our own lives and achieving self-actualization, though we didn't recognize it as such at the time. In 2013, we drove across the country from Florida to our dream home high in the mountains—where we would make substantial changes over the following eleven years. Claudia fell in love with the location the first time I brought her here, and it was the beginning of the hardest yet happiest years of our lives. I can honestly say I swept her off her feet. Both of us, crazy in love, embarked on an amazing adventure—home in the mountains. Claudia was, and still is, my greatest gift from God, and I thank Him every day for her.

It turned out to be exactly what we had hoped: wild, exciting seasonal changes, skiing, snowboarding, kayaking, waterskiing, fishing, thrilling winters, ferocious windstorms (the infamous "Santa Anas"), and fun visits from family and friends eager to share in our "destination resort" lifestyle. All of that awaited us, and we reveled in it. We became incredibly popular as old friends and acquaintances resurfaced, hoping for an invitation to spend a weekend in our mountain paradise.

Bradley kayaking on the lake near our home.

Me and Claudia in Las Vegas in 2013.

Love Relationships: The True Test of Love

So, here we were, off to the races, having a ball—until God slapped us down and said, "Hold on now, just a minute!" A different kind of adventure was about to begin. That was on October 29, 2015—one year and three months after we got married!

That was when we found out what our love was really made of. This was the beginning of the "for better or worse, in sickness and in health" phase of our marriage. It had to be God testing us because no other explanation made sense. Tribulations and hardships in a marriage typically don't start until much later.

At this point, I should mention that it was always Claudia's and my sincere intention to return to Florida regularly, every couple of months, to see our adult children and friends. This need became even more intense as our grandchildren were born.

The real cruelty of the sequence of serious health disasters we endured is that just as we began to recuperate from one challenge and schedule a flight back to Florida, another health crisis would strike. I would get strong and healthy enough to travel again, and sometimes—on the day before a scheduled flight—our plans would be derailed for months.

Birthdays and holidays passed while we were unable to see our adult children and grandchildren, missing countless, irreplaceable family milestones. We watched on FaceTime, frequently from hospital beds, doing our best to be present. The heart-wrenching sorrow this caused, and still causes, especially for Claudia, is something we may never get over. As I write this, Claudia is finally able to go to Florida in a couple of days for a brief visit, but I am not yet cleared to travel.

This is a stark example of the sacrifices that Claudia, in particular, has made out of love for me.

This is Love.

In February 2024, Brad had to abandon his apartment in Seattle, his personal life, and everything else to drive down to our Airbnb near UCLA, where he stayed for four months to help Claudia and me through the transplant process.

This is Love.

In 2017, when I underwent my first open-heart transplant workup, Claudia never left the hospital. Sometimes, she even slept in the same hospital bed as me! She did the same thing years later when I was admitted for emergency gallbladder surgery.

Both times, all the doctors, myself included, stated that they had NEVER seen a spouse so devoted that they would sleep with their partner in the hospital bed (of course, only when my condition permitted it). Every doctor who came into the room in the early morning hours and saw us together said the same thing: "I didn't know these beds could hold two!"

There was one neurologist in particular whom I liked very much, though she had the slightly odd habit of making rounds at 4:00 or 4:30 a.m. She always asked the same questions: "Do you know what the date is? Do you know what hospital you're in?" (I learned to check my phone at 4:00 a.m. in anticipation of this.) I always gave her a good-natured response: "At 4:00 a.m., I don't care what day it is, and I could be on Mars for all I know." We'd laugh together, and she'd move on.

But for Claudia to endure this—having no real bathroom, no decent shower, and no privacy at all, along with me—

This is Love.

After the tumor in my spine was removed, only five months before I needed and received the heart transplant, I was in spinal shock for months. That meant partial loss of control of my bladder and rectal sphincter, along with horrible ongoing chronic pain, residual partial paralysis of my right arm and leg (which has improved somewhat but still lingers), and other neurological symptoms and problems.

Bradley and Claudia, while helping me relearn how to walk and regain other abilities, dealt with countless embarrassing indignities—without hesitation or ever making me feel diminished.

This is Love.

Therefore, this chapter on love and love relationships is less "flowery" or "poetic" than you might expect. Real love means always putting the person you love and their needs ahead of your own. It sounds easy to say, but in extreme, lengthy, unpleasant, and difficult circumstances, it is an exhausting challenge for anyone.

One of the axioms I always taught my sons growing up—and which they love to quote—is that "a gentleman loves himself last." I never dreamed, as I said at the beginning of this book, that all of the axioms and wisdom I shared with them would become so applicable to Claudia and me in our struggle for survival.

There are far too many examples from the past eleven years to describe, but I'm sure I've made my point about what **real love** is.

Now, ask yourself:
• *What kind of love relationship am I in now?*
• *How can I select a partner capable of real love when the worst happens?*

I'll leave it to you to consider, contrast, and compare this real love with infatuation, lust, purely romantic love, and all the other forms of "love" that the human condition is bound to experience—sometimes benefiting, sometimes suffering.

In this vast ocean of humanity and uncertainties, what are you prepared to do to ensure you make the right choices in recognizing **real love**? How do you identify that kind of character in a person? I don't pretend to know all the answers, but just asking the questions is a good start.

Another good starting point is to find prayerful partners equally yoked to God and from families with strong traditions of love and support. Remember those people who don't qualify for a heart (or any other) transplant because they have no family or friends to be there for them for a few months. Also remember the woman who abandoned her husband, packed up in secret, and flew across the country, leaving him stranded and unable to care for himself. You don't want to wind up being that person.

Good spouses are generally also good sons, daughters, parents, siblings, and everything else. Look carefully at how a potential spouse treats their parents and loved ones, especially in times of trouble and hardship. Watch carefully how someone treats servers in restaurants and staff at hotels, etc. Bullying these hardworking service people is a certain red flag for poor character.

Do everything you can to educate yourself and your children about what **real love** is so they, too, can find it. I pray that everyone reading this—especially if you've made it this far—will be successful in finding this kind of love.

This is our "Soul mates for eternity" photo. Sometimes I can't believe that she's actually my wife.

Chapter 14

Altered Perception of Time

By Dr. Rob

Time is the fourth dimension. This concept comes from Albert Einstein's theory of relativity. In this framework, time is combined with the three spatial dimensions—length, width, and height—to form a four-dimensional continuum known as space-time.[11]

Why is this important? Because this concept (and several related theories) mathematically prove that time is not absolute.

Just as matter is composed mostly of empty space (the space between molecules and atoms), there are many concepts that are real but difficult to grasp or accept.

According to the **Block Theory of the Universe** (one of these spin-off theories), all moments in time—past, present, and future—exist simultaneously in the "Block Universe." This theory suggests that time is

---

[11] Steven Gimbel, *Einstein: His Space and Time* (New Haven, CT: Yale University Press, 2015)

like a landscape where all events are laid out, and our **perception** of time flowing is merely a relative way of experiencing the universe.

Stay with me on this—I'm keeping it short, but it's critically important to what we learned while surviving and passing through these NDEs and about prolonging and unifying our lives together. No matter what—not even death!

There is another scientific theory known as **quantum entanglement.** This is a phenomenon in quantum physics where two or more particles become interconnected in such a way that the state of one particle instantly influences the state of the other—no matter how far apart they are, even light-years away. This connection exists **forever**—forward and backward in time.

I like to think of myself and Claudia as quantum particles—our past, present, and future bonded together through space and time.

Time and the NOW Moment

Time can be manipulated through intense, undistracted, hypnotic-like focus on a shared moment experienced together—a **"NOW"** moment as elaborated on in earlier sections.

Claudia and I, in the course of learning to cope with our repeated experiences of losing each other, were fortunate enough to encounter Dr. Deng at UCLA, who helped us realize this concept.

You've probably experienced this yourself. When you're intensely focused on watching a movie, writing, or doing something you love, time seems to stand still. You're surprised at how much time has passed because you were so engrossed in the moment. You think only a few minutes have gone by, but in reality, it's been hours.

That's the **NOW moment.** You've manipulated your perception of time—exactly what we're talking about—except, we're extending this perception **indefinitely.**

Facing Mortality and Love Beyond Time

Of course, no one lives forever, and all of us will die someday. But we can use the power of our brains, the power of prayer, and the power of potent education. When we combine these with an advanced understanding of the incredible force of love, we can evolve to a higher state of appreciating the time we have together as soulmates.

Through this intense focus on the NOW moment, that moment—or day, or year—can last forever because no one and nothing can take that moment away from us. We will always have those NOW moments. This realization has helped remove the fear of losing each other. Claudia and I have learned that we can always hold on to this time together.

I'm not talking about memories or the experience of looking at pictures from shared moments over time. This is something much deeper, more spiritual—seared and burned into our reality because of the intensity, horror, and terror of what we've lived through.

This is love. Our constant focus and awareness of each other have transformed our relationship into a time machine.

Our Gift: Altered Perception of Time

It turns out that throughout the ages, as a consequence of the suffering they endured, people have come across these powerful and liberating concepts. This is the "sausage" that emerged from the "meat grinder" of our experiences, and as I said, it's our gift to you.

This powerful gift—an altered perception of time—extends to your life and loved ones. It has the power to transform your experience of life and death, alleviate your fear of loss, and enrich your experience of love.

I can only hope and pray that I have successfully communicated this message with you.

Chapter 15

Be an Advocate, Fight for Your Life!

By Dr. Rob

In a perfect world, no one would have to fight for their life in a modern hospital in this country—or in any country, for that matter.

But the staggering statistic that inadequate healthcare leads to many preventable deaths in the United States and underscores the necessity to fight for one's life. **Complacency kills.** Sadly, low levels of medical education and a lack of advocacy also lead to preventable deaths. Being alone in the hospital makes you vulnerable. A second set of eyes and ears, when possible and practical, can lead to more questions about your care and someone to research what's going on.

For example, if you have several different IV bags hanging on the "Christmas Tree IV pole," that's fine—but do you know what they are and what they're for? Failing to ask questions, communicate with doctors, or educate yourself about your daily care can be fatal.

AI as a Medical Resource: Use It Wisely

It may surprise you to know that AI sources, like Microsoft's Copilot and ChatGPT, have passed the medical boards—and even the bar exam! If you ask the right questions about your condition, diagnosis (do you know what it is?), and treatment, you'll be better prepared to ask your medical team the right questions and recognize when something is going wrong.

But be careful—AI isn't perfect. The key to successfully using these large language models (LLMs) is to provide detailed information about your situation. Think of the saying, "Garbage in, garbage out." The more context you give, the less the AI has to "guess" or fill in the blanks. While AI can be a valuable, possibly life-saving resource, it isn't foolproof.

Fighting for Your Life: A Personal Lesson

If you know something is going wrong, you have to fight like Hell for your survival. I learned this in the first facility where Claudia and I were treated after the near-fatal head-on collision.

I was left to die for two weeks while the damage to my heart extended through the heart wall due to a failed stent placement. Despite clear signs and symptoms, no one did anything. This was not because of a lack of treatment options but because the attending cardiologist had already decided I was going to die. His antisemitic comments only reinforced his attitude.

Everyone on that cardiology service was intimidated by this attending, and no one cared enough to jeopardize their careers by rocking the boat. They preferred to let me sit there and die. This was the **culture** of that hospital—and sadly, this kind of culture is not unique.

Claudia's desperate, "hysterical" pleas for action (despite her sophisticated medical knowledge) were dismissed and rudely rebuffed. When this happens to you, it's time to leave. Don't be afraid to sign out **against medical advice (AMA)** if you've educated yourself and determined that things are going wrong.

Claudia: Fighting Like a Tiger

Throughout my various illnesses—hip fractures, prostate and spinal tumors, cardiac issues, pneumonia, and emergency gallbladder removal—Claudia fought like a tiger for me when we both knew something was not right.

There were times when I couldn't speak for myself because of medications or sheer illness, exhaustion, and overwhelming pain. During one hospitalization for a left hip fracture (not at UCLA), I coded in the ICU because doctors ignored Claudia's warning that a particular drug was contraindicated and could precipitate **V-tach/V-fib.** They administered the drug anyway, dismissing her as a mouthy, pushy, hysterical female. They ignored our assertions that we had been educated and warned by our UCLA cardiologists about what was and wasn't advisable.

Sure enough, the drug triggered a run of V-tach/V-fib, and I had another near-death experience (NDE) until my implanted defibrillator brought me back. Once again, Claudia had to witness the horror she had tried to prevent.

Misogyny in Medicine: When Women Are Dismissed

It's astounding that in 2025, women are still dismissed, assumed to be ignorant, or treated as "pushy" when they're right all along. In my final hospitalization in Florida—before transferring to UCLA for the transplant—it was Claudia who made the executive decision to sign out AMA and take the daring risk of a commercial flight to UCLA.

The Florida hospital told us there was nothing more they could do for me but refused to discharge me because I was "too unstable." When we asked what we should do, one cardiologist actually said, "I have no opinion on what you should do."

Once again, don't be timid or passive—fight for your life when things are going sideways.

Know Your Rights: Request a Patient Care Advocate

In California and in many other states, you are entitled to request a Patient Care Advocate in the hospital. This is typically an independent nurse or administrator who oversees your care. You can request this advocate by speaking with the Director of Nursing or the Chief of Staff.

Don't be afraid—they work for you! Hospitals, especially private ones, care about their national rankings. When you ring the bells loudly enough and talk to the right people, you'll get a response—and hopefully, better care. Most people don't know this, but now you do.

Do Your Homework: Hospitals Matter

It's easy to say, "Fight for your life!" But you need to know what to do and what tools to use. Hospitals matter. You can research survival rates for different conditions, procedures, and diagnoses by hospital. Choose carefully.

One of my earliest positions was with a massive HMO corporation that dominates Southern and Northern California. I was recruited from New York to California for this position. Their reluctance to perform angiograms—preferring to maximize medications while patients' hearts deteriorated—drove me to resign. They denied access to procedures and medications until patients were nearly critical.

Fortunately, another hospital corporation recruited me and moved me to Florida. The point is simple: hospitals matter, so do your homework.

Doctors Are Usually Not the Problem

The vast majority of doctors—myself included, I hope—are dedicated, caring, and well-meaning. But medical delivery systems are complicated and layered.

After my heart attack, while I was in ICU at the first facility that failed me, I remember pleading with a resident to get answers from his attending or anyone about my plan of care. He responded, "I don't know anything about this. I'm going to be a dermatologist."

It takes courage to be a good doctor in the face of intimidating senior physicians who aren't doing the right thing. Not everyone has that courage.

In Conclusion

A Love Story:
Claudia—My Angel of Love and Life

Claudia had that courage all along—especially when I was too sick or weak to fight for myself. I would be dead many times over if it weren't for her "pushiness" and refusal to take no for an answer. **This is Love.**

She is my **angel of love and life, my soulmate and companion in Christ.** She is the personification and epitome of what it means to advocate for your love and harness the power of faith and love, moving in the same direction and being on the *same focused mission* with shared goals and values. She is my lighthouse in the storm, my moral compass; she has always been powered by her faith in Christ, which was allowed to spread to me!

Yes, like I said in the beginning; this is a **LOVE** story. I give all that I am to her and I still feel unworthy of our love. I would have died ten years ago in 2015, were it not for her.

God is Love and more powerful than death or time. This is not just my opinion, but something I actually lived through. This is the sausage that came out of the proverbial meat grinder. Claudia opened my eyes to what it means to live "in the spirit" with God and the comfort of the secure knowledge of eternal salvation.

In addition to sharing my experiences and trying to impart what I have learned in my life, I want my legacy to be that I learned that finding the right life partner in Christ and connecting with those you love most in a serious, focused, spiritual manner is what matters the most.

Learning to navigate healthcare systems, communicate effectively, question authority in a responsible, educated manner and overcome obstacles relentlessly can be the difference between life and death—and frequently is.

No one lives forever, and despite doing everything right, things still don't always work out well. But it's not over until it's over and until then we have to use all we can to make life go on for ourselves and those who love us.

The strangest thing about everything we have been through is that we never stopped being happy! Things were and still are certainly not always "fun," but we never lost that intense excitement of a new love. I never thought I would find that and wasn't sure I even believed that was possible.

It Is!!

About the Author

Robert Treuherz, MD

Robert Treuherz, MD, has a history of medical practice that spans nearly forty years. Over the course of his career, he has served as: an Internal Medicine physician for the Holy Cross Medical Group in Fort Lauderdale, Florida; a medical director for the Palm Air Medical Center in Pompano Beach, Florida; and a consulting and admitting physician with both 5 Residential Detox in Hollywood, California, and the Care Forward Treatment Center in Beverly Hills.

He was on staff at five different hospitals in South Florida, including Pompano Beach Medical Center, Northridge Medical Center, Holy Cross Medical Group, North Broward Medical Center, and Broward General. Dr. Treuherz has also owned and operated a private practice in Greater San Bernardino and South Florida.

Dr. Treuherz worked for Kaiser Permanente in Riverside, California, where he started the first system wide ethics committee to ensure patient access to needed care. He has also served on Hospital Based Executive

Committees, Peer Review Committees, Medical Records Committees, etc.

He was Board Certified in Internal Medicine in 1996. He was certified in Advanced Trauma Life Support and Advanced Cardiac Life Support.

He laid the foundation for his career in Internal Medicine by completing clinical research with New York Medical College and the Mount Sinai School of Medicine in New York, New York. His primary focus in his medical practice was treating patients in Critical Care settings and general hospital based Internal Medicine.

Dr. Treuherz wrote several articles for *The Mountain News*, a local newspaper based in the San Bernardino County community of Lake Arrowhead. These articles include "Tears of the Mountains" and "Helping Folks Overcome Addiction."

You can contact Dr. Rob at info@twosisterswriting.com.

www.ingramcontent.com/pod-product-compliance
Lightning Source LLC
Chambersburg PA
CBHW070908120626
46546CB00001B/183